The Dream and the Reality of Teaching

Becoming the Best Teacher Students Ever Had

Keen Babbage

ROWMAN & LITTLEFIELD EDUCATION
A division of
ROWMAN & LITTLEFIELD PUBLISHERS, INC.
Lanham • New York • Toronto • Plymouth, UK

Published by Rowman & Littlefield Education
A division of Rowman & Littlefield Publishers, Inc.
A wholly owned subsidiary of The Rowman & Littlefield Publishing Group, Inc.
4501 Forbes Boulevard, Suite 200, Lanham, Maryland 20706
http://www.rowmaneducation.com

Estover Road, Plymouth PL6 7PY, United Kingdom

British Library Cataloguing in Publication Information Available

Library of Congress Cataloging-in-Publication Data
Babbage, Keen J.
  The dream and the reality of teaching / Keen Babbage.
    p. cm.
  ISBN 978-1-61048-017-8 (cloth : alk. paper) -- ISBN 978-1-61048-018-5
(pbk. : alk. paper) -- ISBN 978-1-61048-019-2 (electronic)
  1. Teaching--Vocational guidance. I. Title.
  LB1775.B26 2011
  371.10023--dc22

                                                    2010052908

♾™ The paper used in this publication meets the minimum requirements of
American National Standard for Information Sciences—Permanence of Paper
for Printed Library Materials, ANSI/NISO Z39.48-1992.

Printed in the United States of America

To Judith Keen Johnson Babbage,
my mother and my best teacher

Contents

Acknowledgments

The dear people at Rowman & Littlefield Education are a joy to work with. With this publication, we have worked together on thirteen books. Each experience has been meaningful, rewarding, and educational. Thank you for your perfect professionalism and your treasured friendship.

This book is dedicated to my beloved mother, Judith Keen Johnson Babbage. Two weeks before my mother died in October 2010, I told her that this book would be dedicated to her. She was very pleased with the dedication, yet as a proud mother she was more pleased that her son had completed another book. She was and she will always be our family's best teacher of faith, of love, and of life. My mother made straight-A grades in every class during her college years in the 1940s at the University of Kentucky. She still holds the family grade-point championship.

Introduction

There is no middle ground. There is no compromise. The only honorable options are to be 100 percent a teacher or to do 100 percent other work.

Teaching is not an "I'll give it a try and see what happens" job. Teaching is not "Well, I can always fall back on teaching if nothing else opens up, so I'll get teaching certification just in case I can't find another job." Teaching is not a starter job to do for a few years before moving into another career that will last a lifetime.

If a person approaches his or her first teaching job with the perspective of "Well, I'll see what happens, you know; I'll see how it goes. If I like it and if it's fun, I'll probably stick with it," that person will not succeed as a teacher. First, expecting your job to be fun is to confuse the workplace with an amusement park. No employer and no job owe fun to any worker. Second, there is as much to dislike about the job of teaching as there is to like about the work of teaching. If you quit every job you do not 100 percent like, you will quit many jobs.

If a person approaches his or her first teaching job with the perspective of "My students will learn. I will find a way for every student to learn. I'll do whatever it takes. I will get results," then the imperfections, the frustrations, and the disappointments within the job of teaching do not overpower the achievements, the importance, and the meaning within the work of teaching.

If you are a college student who is considering teaching as a career or who has already decided that teaching will be your career, ask yourself this question: "What must I do to be the best teacher my students will ever have?"

Your response to that question cannot be "Well, I never really expected to be the best teacher my students ever had. You know, I just, well, I mean, teaching looks pretty interesting, and there's really nothing else that interests me." If that is your response, you have two honest alternatives: one, get serious about teaching; and two, quickly meet with your college advisor and change your class schedule to prepare yourself for a career you can commit to fully.

If you are already a teacher, ask yourself a very similar question: "Am I doing everything that is required to be the best teacher my students have ever had?" Your genuine answer to that question is either "yes" based on superior results of your students or "not yet, but every possible improvement is being made so I will soon be and then will forever be the best teacher my students ever have."

If you are a school administrator, your question is "Am I doing everything possible so the teachers in this school become the best teachers our students ever have?" The blunt reality is that school principals work with teachers who have a range of work ethic, dedication, persistence, people skills, teaching skills, and devotion to students. Principals or assistant principals whose highest priority, as measured by how they allocate their time, is to help each teacher become the best teacher the students in that school ever had is a school administrator who remembers that the highest priority of a school—in fact, the purpose of a school—is to cause learning.

Every college student who is considering teaching as a career, every person who is currently teaching, and every school administrator can recall their best teachers. Perhaps it was Ms. Young, who, as your first-grade teacher, invested the extra time and effort to help you learn to read when the reading methods that were working for most students just were not working for you.

Perhaps it was Mr. Wallace, who required you to write, rewrite, rewrite, and rewrite one more time so that eighth-grade essay you entered in a local writing contest truly was your best work. The prize you won in that writing contest was almost as important to you as the personal pride you felt knowing that you had risen to a level of intellectual work that was not easy but that was worth all the effort. The experience Mr. Wallace provided for you can serve as a reminder of and as an inspiration to always provide similar guidance, encouragement, and standards for your students.

You may think of Ms. Brown, who insisted that you learn high school geometry. Triangles, parallel lines, theorems, and proofs in geometry seemed to be a waste of your time. Then Ms. Brown asked you why you refused to become the best soccer player you could be. She knew you were on the high school soccer team. She knew you were a good soccer player. Her question about why you refused to become the best player got much of your attention and some of your anger. Then Ms. Brown showed you all of the geometry on the soccer field. The soccer ball and two soccer players made a triangle. One player moves and the triangle changes. The soccer ball flies in an arc pattern. The field and the goal are full of right angles. The step-by-step thinking and reasoning process in geometry matches the step-by-step thinking and decision-making process in soccer. You mastered geometry, which helped you become a much better soccer player, and you became a very accomplished geometry student who then studied calculus.

Ms. Young, Mr. Wallace, and Ms. Brown have essential insights about teaching. These three masterful teachers were once college students who were thinking about their career options. They chose teaching, and of much importance, teaching also chose them. How did Ms. Young and teaching know that they were made for each other? How do Mr. Wallace and teaching annually renew their commitment to each other? How does Ms. Brown create learning experiences year after year, for unique student after unique student, that inspire great work from students and that also expand Ms. Brown's knowledge of how teaching works best today to cause today's students to learn?

During the thirteen years a student spends in kindergarten through high school, the student becomes aware of some of the work that teachers do. That easily visible part of a teacher's job is possibly 50 percent of the complete job. The student does not see the hours invested in preparing lessons, grading papers, arranging for a guest speaker, computer work, updating grades, attending meetings, attending professional development programs, phone calls with parents or guardians of students, resolving discipline issues, taking graduate school classes, grading more papers, changing Tuesday's lesson plan because of an unexpected, spontaneous learning moment in a class on Monday that must be built upon immediately, writing letters of recommendation for students, answering e-mail, and attending school events, plus much more.

"It can't be that tough. Come on. It's not brain surgery." Yes, it is that tough, and yes, if teaching is done correctly, it is brain surgery. The purpose of a school is to cause learning. The duty of a teacher is to cause learning. Using every possible and proper method of activity, teachers seek to impact brains via learning processes. The work is done in classrooms not in operating rooms. The work is done by a teacher acting alone rather than a surgeon supported by the surgical team. It is tough and it is a form of brain surgery.

This book is being written during the summer of 2010. The high school seniors whom I taught last year graduated four weeks ago. I miss them a lot and I think of them often. The high school juniors whom I taught last year will return for their senior year in six weeks. I am eager to see them again.

Last week, in late June, I went to my school and there was e-mail from a former student. Her high school work was superior, and in her first year of college she had straight-A grades. She has a scholarship that can be renewed annually, so she was asking for an updated letter of recommendation. Her application materials were due in a few days, so I began typing the letter immediately. Wisely, the student had e-mailed her resume so I had updated information. A phone call to her home found a very appreciative mother thanking me for the letter and saying her daughter could come to school to get the letter after her morning job. The plan worked.

The student deserved the letter. The student deserves the scholarship. I am thankful that I could support her college experience. Teachers get to do that. Teachers who realize the unlimited possibilities within their work join the ranks of Ms. Young, Mr. Wallace, and Ms. Brown. Those teachers get to touch lives while also being deeply touched by the life-changing brain surgery, learning-causing work that teaching can be.

The job parts of teaching can be exhausting, frustrating, mundane, counterproductive, and very annoying. The work parts of teaching can add meaning to your life, achievements to your years, purpose to your days, and joy to your moments.

If you are right for teaching and if teaching is right for you, the results can be magnificent. That rightness and whether that rightness exists or can be created for you is the topic of this book.

Stories, characters, case studies, and other examples in this book do not represent any real persons but do represent realistic situations. The stories and people in this book are fictional. The ideas expressed in the stories and through the people are quite real.

Chapter One

Reasons to Be a Teacher, Reasons Not to Be a Teacher

I just love science. It fascinates me. Science was always my favorite subject. Any science. High school was great because there were so many different science classes. College was the best. My professors were brilliant scientists. What could be better for someone who loves science than to teach science?

My grandmother was a teacher. My mother has been a teacher for twenty-nine years. I grew up in a family of teachers. I considered some other jobs, but teaching just seemed to be our family tradition.

My real goal is to be a college football coach. I'll coach high school football for a few years to begin my career. I'll get to know every college football coach I can. Then, when the first college offer comes in, I'll move up to college coaching.

I always thought that teaching would be a family-friendly job. My children will be in school on the same daily schedule that I'll have as a teacher, plus we'll have summers together.

My father is a middle school principal. He's done that about twenty years. I always thought his job looked interesting. So, I'll teach for a few years and then become an assistant principal as fast as possible. Then I'll be a principal the rest of my career. Oh, yeah, I'll be sure to coach several sports while I teach because coaches seem to get chosen for school administration jobs more often.

I had wonderful teachers in elementary school. They were my inspiration to choose teaching as a career. My dream is to be as wonderful for my students as those dear teachers years ago were for me.

To be honest, people have told me to get my teaching certificate because, well, because teaching is a fairly reliable job. It's not like working for a company that can go out of business or that has to lay off a lot of workers. How often do you hear of a school closing? So, with all the economic problems we've had and will probably keep having, I just thought that teaching could provide some job security.

This is not the answer you want to hear, but I really am not all that interested in teaching. I am interested in math. Math just comes easy to me. So majoring in math was an easy decision. My state has some program that pays for your college tuition if you promise to teach math or science. I'll teach for four years, and for each year the state will repay me for one year of my college tuition costs. At the end of those four years I'll have no student loan debt. I'll have a great credit score. I'll have a real resume, and I'll look for some technology company or insurance company that can pay me a lot of money for my math skills.

Teaching interested me because I could start teaching right out of college. At age twenty-two, I was employed as a middle school English teacher. My friends from college were in graduate school. They were paying twenty thousand dollars or more per year for graduate school while I was working and getting paid thirty-five thousand dollars. I can go to graduate school part time and keep working full time.

After I had been a teacher for eight years, I did some serious analysis of my career. I was thirty-one years old and was married. My wife and I had twin boys who were four years old and would begin a full-day preschool program soon. My wife was going back into teaching after being at home with the boys for four years. Our teaching schedules worked for our family. I decided to get certified as a school principal. I could take most of the classes online. One more fact is that I can retire from teaching in twenty-two more years. I'll be fifty-three years old with full retirement pay. I can spend my retirement years with my grandchildren or working part time or playing golf.

I just think that being in a classroom with students is fascinating. I love to create the activities we use in class. I love to hear ideas from students. I really get excited when they ask profound questions or when they give brilliant answers. There are other jobs that I considered, but for me no other job could mean as much as being the teacher who really makes a difference in the lives of students. If you intend to work directly with children or teenagers, you have to be where they are. For me, that means being in the classroom. It's my job, but I see it as more than that. Teaching is what I am supposed to do.

There are many reasons that lead different people to consider becoming a teacher, to actually become a teacher, and then to continue to teach for the decades of a career. Some of the reasons people have for becoming a teacher are more honorable than other reasons. What classroom experiences would students likely have if their teacher is using his high school position as a fast track to a college coaching entry-level job versus if their teacher is absolutely fascinated with and fully concentrating on the process of providing classroom activities that cause meaningful learning?

If you are in college and you are either considering becoming a teacher or you have begun the college program that will certify you to be a teacher, what are your reasons for considering teaching or for selecting teaching?

If you are teaching now, what were the reasons you had as a college student that led you to earn teacher certification, to get a job as a teacher, and to continue doing the work of a teacher? How has your perception of, attitude about, or motivation toward teaching changed during your years of teaching?

Let's create a list of reasons to be a teacher. The first part of the list will be provided and then the reader will complete the list. Please note, some of these reasons in the list are more honorable than some other reasons on the list, but reality is that people who consider teaching and who actually teach have a range of reasons for their career choice.

Some Reasons to Be a Teacher

1. Personal conviction that teaching is the work I am supposed to do.
2. Very good experiences as a volunteer working with children or teenagers.
3. Always hoped to be for students what my best teachers were for me.
4. Fascination with school, with learning, with students.
5. Always wanted to coach sports, and teachers can coach.
6. Get along well with, and relate well to, children and teenagers.
7. The work schedule for each day and for the school year looks good.
8. Attractive retirement plan after thirty years of teaching.
9. One teacher really made a difference in my life, so being in a position to do that for students is important to me.
10. Teaching is just from 8:00 a.m. to 3:00 p.m., so it would be easy to get a second job and make more money.
11. Teaching is fairly secure work. It may not be recession proof, but it is more secure than most jobs.
12. It includes health care insurance as an employment benefit.
13. A lifelong fascination with one particular subject and a hope to help students become fascinated with that subject.
14. Not really interested in, skilled in, or qualified for other jobs.
15. I just like children.
16. My goal is to be the coach of a high school basketball team that wins the state tournament.
17. My high school principal was a great mentor for me. I would like to have that job, so first I have to teach before I can be a principal.
18. I don't want to be a lawyer or a doctor. I'm not very good with math or science. Teaching looks like it would be fun. I pretty much liked school. So, why not? There's nothing else that really interests me very much.
19. It may sound bad, but once you are a teacher it is almost impossible to get fired. I like that kind of job security.

20. It really bothers me that people criticize schools so much. I want to be such a good teacher that people realize that some great work is being done in schools.
21. It's my very personal belief. I've thought about this a lot. I've talked to people who know me well. My family has advised me. I've prayed about it. Everything I know tells me that teaching is the work I should do. I really believe that.
22.
23.
24.

There is no one exclusive perfect reason to become a teacher. The person who just likes children may or may not be able to do the work that causes children to learn. The person who seeks a state high school basketball championship could also get equally superior results in the classroom or could be that coach who expects more of students as athletes than of students as students.

From a variety of reasons to teach could come a variety of results in the classroom; however, there is no one perfect reason to teach from which will come guaranteed results of superior learning by students. There are better, more professional reasons to teach. Total devotion to outstanding classroom instruction that causes every student to learn because in your heart and soul that is what you believe life itself expects of you is a better reason than "Well, I have to teach so I can coach" or "I really like the idea of summer vacation for two or three months every year."

Now, consider the following reasons not to teach. Expand the list with your thoughts, please.

Some Reasons Not to Become a Teacher

1. It just seems like it might be an okay job.
2. I really do not like being with children or teenagers.
3. A few of my teachers were people I never wanted to be like.
4. I never liked school. I could not wait to finish school. Why would I work there and have to go back forever?
5. I really just want to coach, but to coach I have to teach.
6. Children and I just do not relate to each other. Teenagers and I do not relate to each other either.
7. I hear some teachers say it takes seventy or eighty hours a week to do the job well. If I'm going to work that much, it will be at a job that pays a lot more than teaching pays.
8. I cannot invest money in a school if I work there. At a company, I can buy stock and build a big retirement plan.

9. I never had any teachers who acted like they loved their job.
10. You cannot get promoted. There are teachers and there are school principals. Teaching looks like doing the same job year after year. I want a career with some variety and with the chance for many promotions.
11. I keep hearing that school districts have money problems so they lay off teachers or they cut pay and benefits. I'm not interest in those possibilities.
12. What would I teach? There is no subject that is taught in schools that I am an expert in or am all that interested in.
13. My skills are best used elsewhere. I can fix anything. I can build anything.
14. I cannot imagine being around children or teenagers all day long.
15. The teaching part might be good, but there is so much paperwork plus meetings. I prefer a job that has no paperwork.
16. My goal is to own a business. What's teaching got to do with that?
17. I got in trouble a few times in school. I deserved some punishments, but not all of them. I have this strong resentment about how unfairly the teachers and principals treated me.
18. I intend to make a lot more money than teachers make.
19. I never read much good about schools. I do read a lot about problems at schools. Why work at places like that?
20. Most schools are public schools. That means their budgets are limited to what they can get in taxes. I prefer to work some place that does not have to take the lowest bidder on everything.
21. I know a lot of teachers. They complain more than any other people I know. If half of what they say is true, I would never be a teacher.
22. Teaching is working for the government. Everything you do or say has to follow every law, policy, regulation, and procedure. Who wants to work in a place where everything you do is based on some political or legal process. One tiny mistake can destroy your career.
23. I've read about students who falsely accuse their teacher of harassment or other misbehavior. Not one word of the accusation was true, but the teacher's reputation was destroyed. That is not going to happen to me.
24. I had two great teachers. They were at school all the time, early, late, weekends. They were the only great teachers I had. If being a great teacher takes that, I'll do something else.
25. I have never had any reason to think that I should be a teacher.
26.
27.
28.

Please notice that more reasons are listed for not being a teacher than are listed for being a teacher. There is a reason to present the lists that way: the reality of teaching is that the work is more demanding, more complex, more frustrating, more exhausting, more heartbreaking, and more agonizing than is commonly acknowledged. The longer list of reasons not to be a teacher is a reality check. Enter this profession with 100 percent awareness of how magnificent the good teaching experiences can be and of how painful the bad teaching experiences can be. Make the right decision for you, your family, and for students—to teach or not to teach—based on all the idealism you can create and based on all of the reality you can identify.

Avoid teacher's remorse. This is somewhat similar to buyer's remorse. A person decides to move from renting an apartment to purchasing a house. The prospective buyer works for weeks to study the real estate market, to get wise advice, to select a very capable real estate agent, and to get information from several banks. After several months of house hunting, an offer is made and is accepted. The initial excitement is followed by questions and anxiety: Did I pay too much? Can I really afford this? What happens when the house needs repair? Is it really smart to do this? Maybe I should have waited. I'm afraid that this is one big mistake.

Some buyer's anxiety is common. Then the new homeowner moves in, settles in, finds ways to do simple repairs, enjoys having friends visit, gets a tax advantage, and finds that, despite some occasional difficulties, there is much more benefit than difficulty with the properly selected house purchase. The fact that occasional maintenance work or repair work are needed do not mean that the purchase was a mistake.

Avoid teacher's remorse. Know everything you can about all parts of the job of teaching before designing your college years to provide you with teacher certification.

Avoid teacher's remorse. Do not let difficulties in your first, tenth, twentieth, or any year of teaching automatically convince you that teaching is not worth it. Give equal attention to the wonderful experiences and important results that your teaching makes possible. One bad day with one defiant student, one belligerent parent, one unreasonable school administrator, and one interminable meeting are not the parts that define the whole of teaching.

Much that is frustrating, disappointing, annoying, agonizing, and exhausting can be resolved, managed, or reduced. Teaching does have and always will have aspects of the job that are frustrating, disappointing, annoying, agonizing, exhausting, and heartbreaking. Teaching does have and always will have aspects of the job that are exhilarating, inspiring, rewarding, meaningful, and vital.

Some people who become teachers decide to leave the teaching profession and work elsewhere. Some of those people should never have become teachers. Some of those people could have made some changes in what they do, how they do it, and in their thinking that could have made a long teaching career more manageable, more productive, and more fulfilling. Some of those short-term teachers encountered unexpected life changes that required a job change due to factors such as family financial needs, a move to another city, or a rare opportunity that was now or never.

Some people become teachers because they are captivated by, inspired by, and guided by the teaching ideal. These dear people promise themselves that they will be the teacher who touches lives of students in ways that parents, guardians, school administrators, taxpayers, and students hope for. These teachers who are motivated by the ideal can find that their career is in fact filled with many marvelous moments when learning happens as it should, when students surpass what they earlier believed they could achieve, and when the pursuit of the ideal is sufficient encouragement to cope with and to persist through the guaranteed difficulties, aggravations, frustrations, and problems.

Some of the idealistic teachers decide to quit teaching after only a year or two years in the classroom. For them, the moments of ideal achievements were too few and the reality of problems was too discouraging. One conclusion is that some degree of the idealistic approach and attitude can be helpful, but pure idealism is insufficient for managing the totality of the demands that face every teacher.

The work of teaching is very personal and interpersonal. With that thought in mind, let's meet some future, current, and former teachers. As you get to know these teachers, think about whether each of them have more reasons to be a teacher or not to be a teacher.

Hannah Johnson is a seventeen-year-old high school junior who makes very good grades at school, who is quite involved in several school activities, who works about ten hours each week as a babysitter, and whose one and only career ambition has always been to be an elementary school teacher. Hannah is a mentor in a program that matches high school students with a nearby elementary school so the high school students can help provide after-school tutoring to elementary school students who are struggling in math or reading or who are ready to do more advanced academic work than their grade level usually offers.

Hannah loves being a mentor and being a tutor at the elementary school. As Hannah told a reporter from her high school newspaper who wrote an article about the mentoring program,

> I love it. The children are so cute. They are always so glad to see us. There are eight high school mentors who go to Lincoln Elementary School once every two weeks. We really get to know the students. We work on reading or math. They have lots of neat questions about high school. I can't wait to be a teacher. It's the perfect job for me. I'll get to do this type of mentoring and tutoring all day with my own classroom of students. It will be so cool. I'm ready for college, but I'm excited about senior year here. Still, college will prepare me to teach and then I'll go have my own classroom.

Matt Samuels is a senior in college. He will graduate at the end of his fourth year of college, but it has been very difficult to stay on that traditional graduation schedule. Tuition costs have increased 46 percent during the four years that Matt has been in college. He has always had one job and sometimes a second job during the college years because the costs of college required that income. Matt did earn some scholarship support due to outstanding grades in high school and due to continuing to make great grades in college, but the most demanding part of college for Matt has not been the academic work; rather, it has been the costs of higher education.

Matt's plan is to be a middle school teacher. A paper he wrote during his junior year of college when he took a very helpful one-hour seminar class was titled "What Makes You Think You Can Teach?" Matt gave this answer:

> I know I can teach because I have three younger sisters and one younger brother. I've taught them all my life. I volunteer at my church to help with the middle school youth group. I have worked several summers as a camp counselor, and I always concentrated on the eleven- to fourteen-year-old campers. I'm part of a program that sends college students to a local middle school to assist teachers with students who need more individualized work. What makes me think I can teach is the fact that I get good results when I work with students.

Matt did include one concern in his paper.

> It bothers me that, when I visit the middle school where I am a tutor, I hear some negative comments from a few teachers. Some days, I stay after school for an extra hour to help the teacher I work with. I make copies or I get materials from the library or I prepare computer presentations. I always hear a few teachers complain about how uncooperative the students are, how unappreciative the parents are, how invisible the principal is, or how hard the job of teaching is. I was always told to get results, not to make excuses. I hope to be a teacher who gets results.

Matt also hopes to help middle school students realize that, if they intend to go to college, they have to be very serious about that for many years before they go to college. Matt has realized that some college scholarships can be earned by middle school students even though they are several years away from college. Matt plans to be the middle school teacher whose students are academically ready for college and are financially ready for college.

Having watched many friends quit college, Matt has also realized there are ways to prepare for a good career without going to college. He has read a lot about some middle school vocational and technology education programs that prepare students for work that is in demand and pays well. Matt would like to help start or expand a program like that at the middle school where he will teach.

Elizabeth Stephens recently finished her first year of teaching high school English classes to ninth and tenth graders. During her college years, Elizabeth gave very serious thought to a career in law. In fact, she was accepted to an excellent law school. Elizabeth also had a permanent offer to work in her father's real estate management company. Still, Elizabeth had always wanted to be a teacher, and she hoped to be a high school soccer coach. She had played soccer since she was six years old, so teaching high school English and coaching a high school girls soccer team was the most appealing career possibility Elizabeth could imagine.

Elizabeth is not so sure about returning for a second year of high school teaching.

> It's the papers. Day after day, how does anyone keep up with the papers? I have 144 students in my six classes. Three classes meet on A day and three more classes meet on B day according to our block schedule system. If I spend ten minutes per student each week grading papers, that means 1,440 minutes of work at home. That's exactly twenty-four hours. Then we have soccer practices and soccer games. How does anybody keep up with all of this?

Elizabeth has talked with some of the experienced teachers at her school. Their advice was not what she hoped to hear. "It will get better. In a few years, you'll have lesson plans accumulated and you will never have to spend another minute on creating a new lesson plan." When Elizabeth asked what to do when an old lesson plan did not work with new students, she was told, "Oh, it will work well enough. There's no reason to exhaust yourself every year."

Another teacher advised Elizabeth to have the students grade each other's papers. That made no sense to Elizabeth. She is the teacher. She has the college degree. She knows much more about English than her students do, so she needs to grade their papers.

Being the assistant soccer coach had some worthwhile moments and some very frustrating situations. Elizabeth never expected to get so many phone calls and e-mails from parents of soccer players. The complaints were endless. There was never a week in the year when Elizabeth received as many e-mails and telephone calls from parents or guardians who had a question, concern, idea, or problem about the academic performance of their children as she received from parents and guardians who had some comment to make about soccer. The thought went through Elizabeth's mind that working for her father might not be so bad. She also began wondering if applying again to law school could be a good option now. She hated to give up after one frustrating year. She hated the thought that she had failed, yet she was finding few reasons to think that the second year of teaching could be better than the first year had been. As she was having trouble seeing herself teach for a second year, she had more trouble seeing herself teach for thirty years as a career.

Mark Daniels loves to teach. His eight years as a high school physics teacher have been everything he dreamed of, hoped for, and prepared for. The work is harder than he ever expected, but the results are better than he ever expected. There are bad days. There are parts of the job that Mark dislikes. What keeps Mark Daniels coming back to the high school physics classroom day after day and year after year? Students.

Mark became interested in teaching because his parents were teachers. As a child and as a teenager, Mark heard what his parents discussed and then he asked them a lot of questions about school. Mark was determined to be a great student in elementary school, middle school, and in high school. His grades were superior throughout those thirteen years in school, and his attendance at school was almost perfect with only eight absences in thirteen years.

Mark almost changed his career plans during his junior year of college. He took several of the classes that were required to earn certification as a teacher. What those classes taught and what he had learned about teaching from his parents were far apart. His parents talked about very precise, specific actions that worked in their classrooms. The college classes were all about theories of how infants become toddlers who become children who become adolescents who become older teenagers. Mark doubted that these theories of learning or of human growth and development would actually apply when he was a teacher. He had never heard any of his teachers or either of his parents discuss theories. They discussed the reality of their classrooms.

Mark endured the classes about learning theory, teaching theory, child development theories, teenager maturity theories, and several philosophies of education. During the first semester of his senior year of college, Mark took one class about "The Profession" and "The Career of Teaching." He spent almost all of his time that semester as a student teacher. He was in a high school physics classroom finally where the people, the science, the work, the challenges, and the results were quite real. Mark never used any theories as a student teacher, although those concepts were interesting to know. He used scientific activities that intrigued, involved, and excited his students. This was what Mark had envisioned teaching would be.

During his eight years as a high school teacher, Mark has completed a master's degree that included earning certification to be a school counselor. He has begun additional graduate school work that will lead to a doctorate and that will include certification to be a school principal. Whenever Mark is in a graduate school class that leans toward the theoretical, he asks himself when, where, how, why, and for whom he might apply the theory. Usually, he concludes that, as interesting as those theories of counseling, leadership, or management are, what really matters in school is the very real face-to-face work that educators do with students to maximize learning. The pursuit of such learning of, by, and for his students fascinates Mark Daniels as much in his eighth year of teaching as it did in his first year of teaching. Mark expects for that fascination to continue for his lifetime.

For fifteen years, Bethany Abrams has taught fourth or fifth graders. Friends of hers have said to her recently, "Congratulations, Bethany, you are halfway there. Fifteen years down, fifteen years to go. You can retire in fifteen more years. It's all downhill from here."

Bethany thinks otherwise. It has been downhill for about ten years. The first few years of teaching were exciting, and each day seemed to bring some new adventure in Bethany's classroom. Then something changed. Bethany calls it the invasion of the education bureaucracy. More and more, Bethany and the other teachers at her school were told what to do, what to say, when to change from one subject to another, and what was expected by certain days of the school year. Bethany was glad to provide copies of her lesson plans, her detailed analysis of achievement by each student, and her thorough week-to-week instructional design that matched the school district's curriculum guide perfectly. That was not enough.

Bethany and her faculty colleagues were increasingly being required to do everything exactly alike in each classroom of the same grade. The teachers kept telling the principal, "But each student is unique. Each class is unique. We will all get the work done, but we have to be trusted as professionals to do what works with our students." No. The answer was no. The teachers were given an exact master plan for the year, for each month, and for each week, and the master plan was to be followed precisely.

What kept Bethany from changing jobs? During her tenth year of teaching, she and her husband celebrated their eighth anniversary plus the birthdays of their six-year-old and their four-year-old. Bethany's work schedule was family friendly even if Bethany's work circumstances were not Bethany friendly or student friendly.

Bethany kept hoping that the situation would improve. Certainly, the authorities would eventually listen to teachers who kept saying that rigid procedures do not educate unique students. However, if anything, the rigid procedures seemed to get more rigid each year. In the past few years, Bethany found herself just going along with everything and never complaining, never offering an idea, and never asking a question. She knew that complaints, ideas, or questions often went nowhere. She asked herself if she was still a teacher or if she was just a machine in the assembly-line processes imposed on her by people in authority. These processes might train students, but they never teach students. Could Bethany do this for fifteen more years? Her family needed her income. She had to continue. This is not the job she had in mind when she became a teacher.

Lucas James was a teacher, then an assistant principal, a principal, an assistant superintendent, and then, after thirty-three years of an education career, he retired at age fifty-five. Lucas hated retirement, so he took action.

He knew that a law in his state permitted retired teachers to continue collecting their retirement pension and return to teaching if their teaching certification was in an area where there was such a shortage that no other qualified applicant could be found. Lucas identified a middle school that needed an eighth-grade math teacher due to an opening that unexpectedly was created two days before the school year began. He was interviewed immediately and hired faster than the hiring process usually works, but every step was followed properly.

Lucas has an answer:

> Not much that really is important in education has changed in the past thirty or forty years. We spend more money, we have more laws, there are more regulations, there is a lot of technology throughout schools, but those things are not what is really important. You take a teacher who really knows his subject. You put that teacher in a classroom with the books and other supplies he needs. You check in with that teacher often to see if everything is okay or if there is something you can help him with. You give him the freedom and the responsibility to get results. Be sure he is dedicated to students, likes to teach, wants to be with students, works hard, uses a variety of teaching methods, lives up to high professional standards, and never makes excuses; you'll see some wonderful things happen. That's how my best teachers were. They did all of that, and in their classes I worked and I learned because they showed me why I should work and how I could learn.
>
> I know that teachers and principals have endless problems to deal with: students who take drugs; students whose families neglect them; students whose grandparents are responsible for them; and students whose parents give them everything they ask for and then blame the teacher if Johnny does not learn. It's tough, tougher than ever. People who are not in classrooms have no idea of how demanding this work is. Only people in classrooms know how difficult the classroom reality can be, but those same people in classrooms are the only people who actually get to live the dream of every genuine teacher. We dream of touching lives, of inspiring students, of making a lasting difference in the life of students, one at a time. That's why we do this. If your dream is to be a teacher the only place to live that dream is in a classroom.

If you could select the ideal teacher for your seventeen-year-old high school son or daughter to have for political science class today, you would select Marian Jacobs, but that was not always true. Marian has been a teacher for twenty-one years. During the past eleven years, Marian has consistently been selected by students for her school district's hero award. The district encourages high school students to nominate the teacher who has had the most beneficial impact on their education and on their life. The words of one student provide the best explanation of why Marian Jacobs is a hero to so many students.

Ms. Jacobs is always there for us. She gets to school early and is glad to help any student who comes to her classroom with a question. She stays after school and has extra study sessions for us. She comes to our events at school. I've seen her at tennis matches, theater performances, band and orchestra concerts, and I'm sure she goes to a lot more that I don't know about. What's really neat about Ms. Jacobs is that she never gives up and she never lets us give up. She works with you to do whatever it takes for you to learn. She insists that we work and pay attention and turn in everything on time. She is serious about school, but she is serious in a way that shows she cares about us and that she really likes being with us. Everyone does their best work for Ms. Jacobs because we know that Ms. Jacobs always does the best possible work for us.

Comments like those have been made by students to honor Ms. Jacobs throughout the past eleven years. Comments like those were not made about Ms. Jacobs during the first ten years of her teaching career. What changed? Ms. Jacobs will explain:

I had been a teacher for ten years, and each year was worse than the year before. I heard other teachers complain about everything, so I figured this is just bad overall for everyone. It was not really awful. Few people quit. We kept coming back year after year, but you rarely heard of anything great at the school. I wondered if it was worth it to put another twenty years or so into teaching. I was thirty-two years old, so I was young enough to change careers. Also, I was seriously dating the man who would become my husband, and if I was going to change being single to being a wife I thought it might be a good time to change careers if I was ever going to do that.

Well, my husband's mother is a teacher. When my husband—Nick is his name—and I were dating, I got to meet his mother, and she talked about teaching in ways that I never heard people at my school talk. She kept saying how thankful she was that for thirty-two years she got to be a teacher. It was not that she had to teach or that no other jobs were available; it was like she saw being a teacher was a bonus that life had given her. I began to think that way. I get to be a teacher. I get to be the teacher who makes a difference in the lives of students the way my best teachers made in my life years ago.

I wondered why I had never thought of that perspective about teaching before.

Way back in my college classes, which helped me earn the necessary certification to be a teacher, we did not discuss or learn about getting to be a teacher. We learned about the philosophies of education or the theories of learning or the sociological trends that were impacting students.

So, beginning in my eleventh year of teaching, I just thought about teaching differently. Sure, there were policies at our school that I disagreed with. And there were decisions made by the school administrators that I never could understand, but they have pressures on them, and at least, they did listen to input from teachers even if that input had limited impact. And the education laws passed by the state or the U.S. Congress really annoyed me because those people are so far away from what really happens in schools they can't make a realistic decision. Well, I could not change much of those things, but I could always change what my students and I did in the classroom. I could create the overall atmosphere in my classroom. "I get to be a teacher" means that if I take control of the parts of my job that I really can control, then I am the most significant factor in how good my classroom is.

See the difference. It's not the laws or the policies or the regulations. It's not the decisions made by school administrators. It's not the new procedures we are told to follow each year. All of that is part of any system. Businesses have policies. Schools have policies. Laws are everywhere. I can comply with every requirement of my school and still be in control of what happens in my classroom. Even when there is something I am required to do or forced to do, the attitude in my classroom about doing that is up to me. I like to control what my students and I do plus how we do it, but if someone else controls the what I can still control the how.

Do I say to my students, "We have this survey we have to hurry up and finish for something the state is making us do"? Or do I say, "Today we get to tell the people in state government what we think. This is democracy in action. As you complete this survey, you are using a First Amendment right. You are also involved in life, liberty, and the pursuit of happiness. Let's start"?

So, I do not ignore problems or frustrations or disappointments at school. I've kept a list of what I would change if I were a principal, and if I ever get that job, I'll put that long list to good use. Even then, some people will complain or disagree. And I would have a chain of command giving me instructions I might not agree with. For now, I get to teach, and I really can create the atmosphere in my classroom; I really can create wonderful opportunities for the students in my classes. I have eleven years of good results to support the idea that, when I think and work with the approach that "I get to be a teacher," the experience for students and for their teacher is just magnificent.

There is much to think about and to learn from the experiences of Hannah Johnson, Matt Samuels, Elizabeth Stephens, Mark Daniels, Bethany Abrams, Lucas James, and Marian Jacobs. Let's pause for a few moments of reflection. What ideas, insights, problems, joys, dreams, and realities stand out as you think about the seven people we just met?

The topic of time was a part of what we heard from some of those teachers. The reality is that teachers spend almost all of their time at school with children or teenagers. Is that your ideal work environment? The answer must be yes if you are to succeed as a teacher. It is absolutely unacceptable to think, "Well, teaching would be a lot better if those youngsters would act like adults." Those youngsters are—this should not be a surprise—young. You get to teach them what they need to know today and what they will apply throughout their adult years. If you prefer to work all day with adults, being a teacher in a classroom is not the job for you.

Time was also mentioned in terms of the hours that some teachers must invest in their work in addition to the seven or eight hours daily with students. Some teachers arrive at school a few minutes before classes begin and leave in the afternoon a few minutes after classes end. Other teachers arrive an hour or more before classes begin and remain at school for hours after the school day ends for students. Some teachers spend ten, twenty, or thirty hours each week doing schoolwork at home. Some other teachers rarely do schoolwork at home. One teacher cannot control the number of hours that another teacher invests in school. Can you accept that you might work seventy hours a week as a teacher and get paid less than another teacher at your school who works forty hours per week? Can you accept that your pay is not impacted by the number of hours you invest in the job or in the results you get with your students? Such workplace circumstances are parts of the reality of teaching. For some people, those realities may reduce the appeal of the dream of teaching. For other people, the dream of teaching is more important than those workplace realities. Which group of people are you in?

Some teachers never miss a day of school or quite rarely miss a day of school. Some other teachers have a very obvious habit of being absent on Friday as long as they have remaining sick days to use. While you make the commitment to arrive at school early every day, stay at school late each day, return papers to students within two days, never give the students busy work, and always design meaningful instructional activities for your students, another teacher could be doing the opposite. Will that frustrate you such that it impacts your attitude about teaching and such that it impacts how you teach? Will you be able to rise above that workplace reality and maintain your commitment to your standards, your integrity, your students, and your promise to be a great teacher?

What will you do on the days when nothing goes right in your classes; you are exhausted; the computer does not work; the copy machine does not work; several students who are usually very reliable do not turn in a major homework project; you get late notice about a meeting after school that you must attend; and a fire drill practice occurs during a class that was taking a very important test? On that day, can you still think, believe, and work according to "I get to be a teacher," or is the possibility of such a day a reason for you to think that another job could be a better match for your skills, temperament, goals, and life?

There are many reasons that can convince a person to be a teacher. There are many reasons that can convince a person not to become a teacher. Which of those lists is longer for you? Even if not the longer list, which of those lists is more compelling for you?

Bottom line: do the reasons to be a teacher make a stronger case for you, or do the reasons not to be a teacher make a stronger case? If you are already involved in teaching, the bottom line changes to, do the reasons to continue to be a teacher make a stronger case for you, or do the reasons to no longer be a teacher make a stronger case for you?

In the next chapter, we further explore the realistic work that is required to fully live the dream of teaching.

Chapter Two

The Work of Teaching Requires Heart, Mind, Body, and Soul

Jonathan Bethel had to give the question he was being asked a lot of thought. Throughout his thirteen years of teaching middle school health and physical education classes, he had not been asked this question.

Paul Gabriel, a sophomore at a university in the city where Jonathan Bethel teaches, was taking an introduction to teaching class, and one requirement of the class was to spend twenty hours during the semester observing a teacher doing his or her work at school. Another requirement was to interview that teacher and write a paper that summarized the insights from the interview, including reflections based on the twenty hours of observations.

Paul's first question in interviewing Jonathan was "If you had it to do over again, knowing what you know now, would you decide again to be a teacher?" Paul knew to provide time for the question to be thought about, but there were more moments of silence than he had expected.

Finally, Jonathan replied,

That is such an important question. It will take a very long answer to completely explain my thoughts. The short answer is yes. The long answer is filled with details. Here goes.

Teaching is more than my job. Teaching is, well, teaching is the work I do so my talents are applied toward my concerns. This is what I mean. I'm a good teacher. I'll be great at teaching someday, but I've worked really hard to be good and to make improvements each year. You don't work that hard or seek to make improvements in anything unless it really matters to you. Teaching really matters to me, that is, teaching well really matters to me.

Why? Many reasons. I had a favorite teacher when I was in elementary school. I was really struggling with arithmetic. I could add and subtract, but multiplication and division were beyond me. Fractions were the worst. This teacher—Mr. Goshen was his name—heard me say one Monday that my baseball team had won a tournament over the weekend. The next thing I knew, Mr. Goshen—his first name was Jacob—gave me all kinds of baseball math problems to solve. I calculated batting averages, earned run averages, average attendance at major league baseball parks, all kinds of statistics for my neighborhood team, and then eventually statistics for my favorite professional teams.

When I finished all of those baseball calculations, Mr. Goshen asked me to explain what all of the numbers meant, so I told him. Then he directed me to point out to him where, in all of those calculations, I had used addition, subtraction, multiplication, and division. I showed him so many places where those math functions were used that I was beginning to think that baseball was more about math than about getting hits and scoring runs.

I was fortunate to have many high-quality teachers during my school years. And there were a few teachers who we could all tell either hated their job or did not like students or who really wanted to do some other job but could not make that happen. Overall, I had good teachers, but Mr. Goshen was the best. He showed me that math was real. It's funny. I actually played baseball at my college, and I think my mathematical understanding of the game was an advantage that earned me as much playing time as my athletic skills did. I could always analyze the baseball statistics of a game, of a season, of any player, and figure out what the problem was or what was working best.

When I decided in my junior year of college to become a teacher, the big influence on that decision was the impact that Mr. Goshen had on my life. I decided to put myself in the position where I could do for students what Mr. Goshen did for me.

So, yes, if I had it to do over again, I would decide to be a middle school health and physical education teacher. Now, I know much more about teaching after doing this work for thirteen years than I did when I made my career decision. My knowledge of teaching has increased. What I do in the classroom changes each year to apply the unique skills of my current students and to find the best ways to get this year's students to do their most outstanding work. What has not changed is my daily determination to be Mr. Goshen for my students. Not to imitate him but to have the same commitment to students that he had and to touch their lives like he impacted my life.

Paul's complete interview with Mr. Bethel included several other questions:

- "What are your biggest frustrations with being a teacher?"
- "What would you change about your school if you could make one change?"
- "What advice would you give to college students who are thinking about becoming teachers?"
- "What advice would you give to people who are already in a career but who are thinking about a career change into teaching?"

- "What's the best part of teaching that many people do not realize is so good?"

Mr. Bethel's answer to that last question provides a clear look into more of his fundamental beliefs about teaching:

> It is very difficult work. Very difficult, but also very possible to succeed in if you care enough, work enough, think enough, persist enough, get lots of advice, and keep the promise you originally made to yourself to be the type of teacher for your students that your best teacher was for you.

> Teaching is hard work. I teach six classes every day. I have about 150 or more students daily. They bring their talents and their problems, their goals and their failures. They bring to my class their knowledge and their need to learn much more than they know so far. I can't think of a more fascinating challenge.

> Other people love to work with computers or with finances or with politics or with medical care. Those are important tasks, but those tasks do not fascinate me and certainly do not inspire me. Teaching inspires me. Students fascinate me. It is never an easy job to do, but it is always an important job. So when teaching gets extremely difficult, I don't run away from it. I run closer to it. Those difficulties challenge me to become a better teacher. I love the successes, and it is good to have a calm day occasionally when everything goes well, but those days are rare. I expect challenges because, in the midst of 150 middle school students, challenges and difficulties are guaranteed. That means I am needed. So that's part of what is good about teaching that most people may not realize.

Paul expressed sincere appreciation to Jonathan Bethel for the opportunity to observe his classes and to ask him questions. The twenty hours of observation were over, and the interview was complete. As Paul reflected on what he had seen and heard, this thought emerged: "Jonathan Bethel is a relentless dreamer. He began his teaching career with a dream to profoundly touch the lives of students. That dream is as vibrant now as it was when he began teaching thirteen years ago. The work is difficult and challenging, but the commitment to the dream is stronger than the force of any obstacle. A dream combined with unstoppable work will equal results."

One of Paul's friends is taking the same introduction to teaching class. Martha Salem hopes to become a high school Spanish teacher. She has observed in Joe Peterson's Spanish 1, 2, and 3 classes for a total of twenty hours. She has arranged to meet with Mr. Peterson during his planning period to conduct the interview. She asks the same questions that Paul asked so the class would have the research consistency of identical questions, yet each student could add more questions to satisfy a personal curiosity about teaching or to build on something unique within their observation experience. Mr. Peterson has sixteen years of teaching experience.

Martha had several unique questions for Mr. Peterson. The question she was most eager to ask was this: "Do you think that all students should be required to stay in high school until they graduate?" Martha had done much research on the high school dropout problem, and she was convinced that the graduation rate could increase. The ideal graduation rate, Martha thought, would be 100 percent, although getting to that goal would take more effort, ideas, and resources than were currently available. Martha just thought that it is right for each student to complete high school, so any graduation rate less than 100 percent was unacceptable to her.

Mr. Peterson was ready to reply.

100 percent? Everyone? That will never happen. Never. No way. It is impossible. Waste of time to try. Who comes up with these ideas? Probably people who never set foot in a school. People who campaign for some elected office or who call up some radio talk show or who work for one of those think tanks. We already give 100 percent of the students the opportunity to graduate from high school. Most of them accept that opportunity, but others reject it.

Here's an example. One student comes to me in May of his senior year. He needs to pass my class to earn enough credits to graduate. Truth is, he needs to pass every class to graduate. So, in May of his senior year, with graduation three weeks away, he asks me how he can get his grade up enough to pass. I don't want to be rude to the student, but his average in the class was 35 percent. He had 770 points out of 2,200 points possible this semester. He missed tests months earlier and never made them up. The policy says it's too late now. Same with homework he never turned in. He has missed my class thirty-one times this semester; almost all of those were from skipping school. He can't pass. He will not graduate. I asked his other teachers and the numbers are about the same in their classes.

I did my job for that student. I called his family. I e-mailed his family. I took attendance accurately, so the skipping should have been noticed by the people who check those things. The student had his chance. And about 20 percent or so of the students who start high school do not finish high school for various reasons, some like the boy who tried to make up in May for what he chose not to do in January, February, March, and April. I did my job. The student did not do his job.

Martha asked all of the other required questions, plus several questions she had created. She then included one more question in response to what Mr. Peterson had said so often throughout his answers. "You refer to teaching as your job. You have mentioned that you did your job or that your job requirements were always completed or that every official evaluation of your teaching concluded that you satisfactorily met the standards of the job. Do you ever think of teaching as more than a job?"

Mr. Peterson must have been asked that question before because he gave more than an answer; he spoke as an attorney in the courtroom would.

More than a job? Certainly not less than a job. People are hired to teach. They sign a contract. They come to school. They do their job. They get paid. Teaching is a job.

Now I know that some people disagree with me. Some people say that teaching is the most important of all professions because teachers touch the future when they teach the students of today. That's a lovely thought, but it does not change the fact that teaching is a job.

What is a job? It is what a person is paid to do. The dentist's job is to fix your teeth. He does that and he gets paid. All you expect from him is for your teeth to get fixed. A mechanic repairs your car and he gets paid. His job is to fix cars. A person who designs websites gets paid to put your company information on the computer screen. That is her job and she gets paid.

My job is to teach. I am required to show up, take my students through the approved curriculum, maintain all grades and other records, complete other reasonable duties as assigned, and then I get paid. Sounds like a job, doesn't it?

I've heard all the crusaders and politicians and dreamers say that teaching is the way we improve our society. I think more effective law enforcement, border security, and lower taxes would be how we improve our society. I do my job. My job is to teach. That means I take my students through the curriculum one day at a time. Some students make the effort to go with me through the curriculum. Other students don't. Either way, I do my job.

Martha thanked Mr. Peterson for his time and for the chance to visit his classes. Mr. Peterson replied, "You are welcome. I hope you get the teaching job you want right after you graduate from college. Let me know if I can ever help."

Martha smiled and walked out of the school toward her car. She thought to herself, "I'll get the teaching job. You can count on that. But I'll never think of it or treat it just as a job. My worst teachers were, what can I call them, 'jobbers.' My best teachers put their heart and soul into teaching and made it much more than any job can ever be. Maybe Mr. Peterson can come observe in my classroom someday and realize then what he is missing."

Jonathan Bethel and Joe Peterson are both teachers; however, their understanding of what a teacher does and how a teacher does that work is vastly different. Jonathan Bethel realized what the work of a teacher could be when his best teacher, Mr. Goshen, taught him in ways that challenged him, inspired him, enthused him, energized him, guided him, and enabled him to realize the benefits, fascination, meaning, importance, and application of math.

Mr. Peterson was not taught by Jacob Goshen. If Mr. Peterson was taught by someone whose perception of teaching, attitude about teaching, and teaching methods were similar to Jacob Goshen's, it did not impact Mr. Peterson the way Jonathan Bethel was impacted by his experiences in Mr. Goshen's math classroom.

Is Joe Peterson opposed to the teaching concept that Jonathan Bethel advocates? Is Joe Peterson convinced that the only way, the right way, the best way, to view teaching is that a teacher has a finite job to do, not an infinite dream to pursue? Does the Joe Peterson jobber approach have a basis in serious reality or in hardened cynicism? Does the Jonathan Bethel dreamer approach have a basis in enlightened facts or in elusive fantasy?

What would be the result of combining the best aspects of Mr. Peterson's serious reality and the best aspects of Mr. Bethel's enlightened facts? Could that combination create a teaching model that directly confronts reality yet never sees today's reality as a limit on what could be accomplished. To explore that possibility, it will help to more fully understand the thoughts of Joe Peterson and Jonathan Bethel.

Joe Peterson prides himself on being a realist. He is a realist on purpose. He put his realist thoughts into a graduate school paper he wrote some years ago when he was earning a degree that included certification to be a school administrator. The most important paragraphs of his paper are below and will provide more insights into how Joe Peterson developed his perception toward the job of teaching.

"THE REALITY OF TEACHING," BY JOE PETERSON

Teaching is not something that I have a philosophy about. Philosophy does not get the papers graded for my classes. Philosophy does not get defiant students to finally do what they should have done in the first place. Philosophy does not get lesson plans made, grades entered in the computer, or paperwork completed to meet a deadline the school principal established. Philosophy is something to think about. Teaching is something to do.

Of course, I want all of my students to learn, succeed, behave, and complete their education. I do my part to help make that happen. It is my responsibility, my job, to do my part to help make that happen. It is also the responsibility of the student and the job of the student to do his or her part. Students who do exactly what I tell them to do will learn the Spanish language because what I tell them to do is what my education and my experience have shown me gets results.

For students who refuse to do exactly what I tell them to do, they learn less, they make lower grades, and they may fail the class. I follow the school policies precisely about students getting partial credit for turning in work late and about students making up tests within a certain time limit. I do not bend those rules for anyone, which means that everyone has the same opportunity with no exceptions. Everyone is treated the same, so everyone is treated equally.

Our school provides some second-chance programs for students. When students fail a class in the first semester, they can take an online tutorial class during the winter break to get caught up, and then the first day of the second semester they have to be at school at seven in the morning to take an exam on the computer. If they make a grade of 75 percent or higher on that exam, they get a passing grade for the first semester in that class. They can use this second-chance plan for up to three classes per semester. They can do the same thing in June for the second semester except in their senior year.

I know that the second-chance plan sounds like it is very helpful to students. There is a problem. Some students fail a class—or two classes or three classes—on purpose. Their explanation is that doing the online tutorial and the one-hour exam on the computer is a much easier plan than doing the work in class for an entire semester. What are we teaching them when we set up a system that gives them an easy way out of doing the real work they should do? Will their employer give them second chances like this? Will life give them second chances like this?

Through the many years of my teaching career, I have had many sincere discussions and disagreements with other teachers who always tell me that I am too rigid, too unwilling to compromise, too insistent that everything is done exactly according to what the rules and the procedures tell us to follow. I tell them that if I did anything more or less than what the rules and the procedures require, it would be confusing to my students. I think it is very helpful to students when they know exactly what is required and when they know that zero exceptions will be made.

It is true that in my early years of teaching I was very flexible. I gave students second chances, third chances, fourth chances, and more. I was willing to try every new idea that the state's department of education suggested or that the local school district wanted to try. The principal back then knew that any innovative pilot program could be tried in my classes. I was willing to experiment with just about anything in hopes that the best teaching system could be found.

The results were awful. Students were confused because what we did changed so much. Students missed due dates for homework because they could still get up to 75 percent credit for late work. They knew that 75 percent credit was a passing grade, so why hurry to be on time? They did not perceive the second chance as an occasional way to make up for missing a deadline. They saw the second chance as a way of life. The solution was obvious. Second chances were eliminated. Blunt, strict rules were clearly communicated and were fully enforced.

Whatever happened to all of those innovations and pilot programs that came from the state's department of education, from the local school district, or from the school administrators? A few, a very few, of them worked and are still in use, but most of them failed. It became obvious to me that, when politics imposes changes on schools, the results are rarely good for students and teachers. It also became obvious that most education innovations are trendy, expensive fads that make money for someone or that advance a career for someone but that do little or no good for students and teachers.

The reality of teaching is that teachers must deal with a very demanding reality in their classroom every day. This job can be done very effectively and very efficiently if it is done as a job in which the teacher realistically does what can be done. This realistic teacher cannot be our nation's tool for solving every problem children and teenagers face. The reality is that we have a curriculum students need to learn. I will do my part 100 percent to help the students learn. If the students do their part 100 percent, the results are what was intended. If the students do not fulfill their duties, it becomes the job of someone else to deal with that. Parents, guardians, school counselors, school administrators, social workers, juvenile justice officials, and mentors in the community can help. I am glad to do my job, but it is not possible for any teacher to do everyone's job. That is the reality of teaching.

Is Mr. Peterson right about the reality of teaching? Do some of his ideas have merit while others are not valid? Is his reality of teaching a reasonable approach, or is it a way to rationalize the adjustments he has made? What type of school would exist if every teacher at the school used Joe Peterson's approach? What achievements would occur? What achievements would not occur? What problems would be prevented? What problems would be solved? What learning experiences would students have? What career experiences would teachers have? What statements could the school's principal make about the educational programs and processes at the school?

Jonathan Bethel has taken graduate school classes. He has earned certification as a school counselor and as a school principal as he earned two graduate degrees. In one graduate school class that Jonathan took (the course had the intriguing name of "Solving the Real Problems in Schools"), he wrote a reflective paper on the topic "What Do You Do About a Student Who Does No Work?" Jonathan designed his paper to provide specific actions that could be used. As you read his paper, evaluate whether the recommended actions could get results. Also, determine what the ideas in this paper reveal about Mr. Bethel's overall understanding of what a teacher can accomplish.

"WHAT DO YOU DO ABOUT A STUDENT WHO DOES NO WORK?" BY JONATHAN BETHEL

1. Persist. It is frustrating, aggravating, annoying, unfair, impolite, and exhausting when a student stubbornly and defiantly refuses to do schoolwork. Still, we must persist. We have the professional, ethical, and personal responsibility to persist.

2. Use every available human resource. Perhaps the student is doing some work in another class—find out what is working there. Perhaps the student is doing good work in a nonacademic part of school—find out what is working there. Perhaps the student is very conscientious at a part-time job—get ideas from the employer. The student might be involved in a community activity—find ways to connect that with school. There may be another current teacher, a school counselor, a school administrator, a teacher who worked with the student years ago, a coach, or a community member who has a strong rapport with the student—recruit those people to help.

3. Read the student's cumulative folder. Did the student do better in elementary school and then something happened? Did the student do better in elementary school and in middle school but never really made a successful transition to high school? Did the family move? Has the student changed schools several times? Are there some comments from teachers in years past that offer some insights? Are there some testing scores that give some useful information?

4. When the student does any work at all, is there something in that work that can be acknowledged favorably? We get more of what we reward. Some students get in habits and in patterns. Students who make A grades often expect themselves to make A grades. The same is often true for students who make other grades. It can take a monumental effort to break out of bad habits and patterns. A few years ago, we noticed that we did a lot for students who made failing grades to get them up to passing. We did a lot to reward the honor roll students. Students with 2.0 to 2.99 C averages did not fit in either category. We decided that, for anyone in that 2.0–2.99 GPA range who improved their GPA by 0.5—as going from 2.1 to 2.6—there would be some rewards. Several students improved more than 0.5, and all of them who improved began to see themselves as capable of more than their habits had allowed them to settle for.

5. Look for small victories. Students in high school who do no work are probably used to doing no work. They will not go from doing no work to doing all work instantly. When they go from no work to some work, that merits some acknowledgment. I recall the junior I repeatedly worked with last year because his schoolwork was unacceptable and his behavior was

worse. One day, much to my amazement, he answered a question I asked him with "yes, sir." As soon as possible, I called his mother to tell her how polite he had been. I had called her several other times before with bad news. She was thrilled to hear good news. She shared her joy with her son. He did not become an instant angel, but he did improve. A few days ago, that same student and I had a wonderful conversation about his college plans. He smiled. He was polite. He was appreciative. It began with a small victory, and it took much persistence. Progress was not consistent each day, but progress was made often enough to get some favorable results eventually.

6. Alternative programs are sometimes needed. Some students just are not going to respond to any of the offerings that can be provided in a school that serves a wide range of students from the senior who will earn a full scholarship to college to the sophomore who is seriously considering dropping out. Alternative school programs that have different schedules, different curriculum options, different uses of computer tutorials, and different locations serve the growing need for alternative education program options. For students who are court involved, communities and the state may need to create new options that combine juvenile justice and education.

7. Keeping in touch with families can help with some students. I have been encouraged with the results this year when I mailed a letter to the parents/guardians of students in my classes. It was not a report card or a progress report; rather, it was an individualized update (a) about the academic grade with an explanation for why it was good or bad; (b) about the behavior with an explanation for what was causing that to be good or bad; and (c) about how to get information about the class from my Web page. This did not solve all problems, but it certainly did solve some. If the student was doing good work and behaving well, the families really appreciated the good news. Sometimes, I call parents/guardians to tell them about great test grades or of great work on projects, or to tell them of improvement. The parents/guardians always appreciate the information. Sometimes, students tell each other about such calls, and it can impact the overall atmosphere or attitude in a class.

8. Trade ideas with colleagues. Each day in each school, teachers are doing good work, but the other teachers in that school do not get to see that work and rarely hear about it. Also, our profession has many good organizations, publications, and books that are sources of ideas. Sure, some of those organizations, publications, and books may not be worth much time, but others are beneficial. Selectively use those resources.

9. There can be power in choice. One teacher I know had students do a career history project. They select the career they are interested in and they research that career's history. If you would like to be a dentist, you

research the history of dentistry in this country. If you would like to be a computer technician, you research the history of computers and related fields. The project combines history with the career choice of each student. The project also gives students a required amount of research but leaves some format options of how they present the information. Format choices appeal to the creativity preferences of students. As students get to help create their projects, they become more supportive of the work itself.

10. Persist. We return to the idea with which we began. The student who refuses to do the work we assign must know that we will never stop doing our work for and with that student.

11. Overall, be the teacher you promised yourself you would be when you first chose teaching as your career. Different people select teaching for a variety of reasons, but among the reasons on almost every person's list is some statement of intending to make a difference in the lives of students. No college student who is preparing for a teaching career says to themselves, "I intend to spend thirty years in an ordinary classroom passing out pointless worksheets each day and telling struggling students to work harder while I then tell successful students to wait for everyone else to catch up." We choose teaching and teaching chooses us because, even though we know how difficult the work will be, we are the people who can conquer that difficulty with our creativity, energy, idealism, relentless effort, devotion to students, and determination to be the teacher we promised ourselves we would be.

It is intentional and obvious that missing from Mr. Bethel's approach to students who do not work is any reference to him, as the teacher, giving the students an opportunity to learn, but the students did not accept their duty to make the most of the opportunity. Is Mr. Bethel's persistence honorable? Is Mr. Bethel doing too much for his students?

Clearly, Mr. Bethel dreams of all students learning, achieving, and succeeding. To implement that dream, he accepts the challenge, responsibility, and adventure of finding or creating the actions he can take as a teacher to cause the desired learning by each student. Mr. Bethel knows that he is employed to do the job of teaching; yet, his understanding of teaching goes far beyond what the common job description asks or requires.

Is Mr. Bethel right about thinking that the dreams of idealistic teachers are worth pursuing and could come true? Do some of his ideas have merit while others are not valid? Is his concept of teaching a reasonable approach, or is it asking too much of himself and of what a school can help him accomplish?

What type of school would exist if every teacher used Jonathan Bethel's approach? What achievements would occur? What achievements would not occur? What problems could be prevented? What problems could be solved?

What learning experiences would students have? What career experiences would teachers have? What statements could the school's principal make about the educational program and processes at the school? What problems would endure?

What similarities do you notice in the ideas of Mr. Peterson's paper and in the ideas of Mr. Bethel's paper? What differences do you notice in the ideas of the two papers? Which approach more closely matches your concept of teaching? What beneficial idea could you take from the other approach, or are you completely opposed to that other approach?

What questions would you like to ask Mr. Bethel about his dream of teaching and how that dream impacts what he does in his classroom with students? Space is provided for the reader to list those questions:

1.

2.

3.

4.

5.

What questions would you like to ask Mr. Peterson about his thoughts about the reality of the job of teaching and how that job reality impacts what he does in his classroom with students? Space is provided for the reader to list those questions:

1.

2.

3.

4.

5.

Sometimes truth is in the middle. Between too much and not enough can, in some parts of life, be found a moderate middle that maximizes results.

For example, a person who gets no exercise is advised by her physician to gradually begin an exercise program. The goal is to work up to forty-five minutes of pulse-increasing physical exercise daily. This forty-three-year-old named Ellen needs to lose some weight and pay close attention to her some-what elevated blood pressure levels.

Ellen decides that if a little amount of exercise is good and a moderate amount of exercise is better, then the best plan must be the most exercise possible. She goes from zero exercise to one hour per day within two weeks. After two more weeks, she is up to ninety minutes of exercise per day. She then tries two separate one-hour exercise sessions daily, and after three days, has aches and pains that force her back to zero exercise.

For Ellen, the conclusion was that too much exercise was bad and that no exercise was bad. Somewhere in the middle, a moderate amount of daily exercise is the ideal plan.

Is there a midpoint between Mr. Bethel's dream of teaching and Mr. Peterson's job reality of teaching that could take the best parts of those two approaches and surpass what either approach alone could achieve? Ruth Matthews is a good person to provide an answer.

Ruth is in her twenty-third year as an educator. Ruth has three favorite days each year: Christmas, her wedding anniversary, and the first day of the school year. Ruth is thrilled each August when students arrive for the beginning of the new school year. There is an excitement level and a sense of optimism on that day that Ruth both absorbs and radiates. She does everything possible to maintain that excitement and that optimism throughout the entire school year.

Although the first day of the school year is highly valued by Mrs. Matthews, there are two other days each year that are more important to her. Ruth and her husband Paul Matthews have been married for twenty-four years. Their devotion to each other and to their twenty-one-year-old twin daughters has been rewarded with a loving, joyous, meaningful, and able-to-endure-difficulties family life. The annual celebration of the Matthews' anniversary is Ruth's second favorite day of each year.

For Ruth, Paul, and their daughters, Julie and Katie, Christmas is the best day and the most important day of every year. The Matthews family has always given their Christian faith the highest priority. For Ruth, faith, family, and education are her three top priorities in order of importance.

Ruth completed her master's degree during her first year of marriage while Paul was beginning his career as a high school teacher. Ruth and Paul had fascinating conversations during that year as the events of the day from Paul's high school tenth-grade world history class were evaluated against the concepts that Ruth was studying in her master's with Initial Certification program.

Ruth had majored in biology during her college years, and as a senior in college decided to become a middle school teacher. Why? Her experience as a camp counselor during the summer after her junior year of college showed her that working with thirteen-year-olds was just as adventurous as working with biology experiments. Teaching middle school would enable her to combine those endeavors. Her master's degree program included all teacher certification requirements in addition to highly sophisticated work in biology.

Throughout their careers, Ruth and Paul have had a variety of positions in education. Paul has taught tenth-grade world history, has been an academic team coach for his high school, has served as academic dean at that high school, and is now one of the assistant principals at the high school. Paul has worked for twenty-four years at the same high school and in recent years has welcomed to the school several children of students he taught twenty-four years ago. Those students often ask Paul to tell them stories about their parents.

Ruth has worked in the same school district as Paul, but she has been in five different positions during her twenty-three years. She taught middle school biology for five years. Then, for three years, she taught biology in a high school magnet program with a very advanced science emphasis. She then served as the director of that magnet program for three years. Along the way, she had earned another graduate school degree that included certification as a school principal. She worked for five years as a middle school assistant principal. During the past seven years, Ruth has been a middle school principal. She may continue in this job until retirement, although she has an interest in returning to high school, and the idea of being a high school principal as the final step of her varied career has much appeal to Ruth.

Ruth and Paul have often talked about writing a book based on their career experiences. Their book idea is to contrast what they learned in college or graduate school as they prepared for a career in education versus what their actual career experiences have shown them they need to know to succeed in their career. Paul likes the book idea but says he will not have enough time to write that much until he retires. Ruth is more interested in the book idea and is determined to write the book before she completes her twenty-fourth year in education. She hopes to dedicate the book to Paul and to give him the first copy of the book on their twenty-fifth wedding anniversary.

Part of what has been so rewarding to Ruth during her years as a school administrator has been the vast learning she has gained from being in the classrooms of several hundred teachers. Few teachers get to observe other teachers teach. Ruth has observed, talked to, met with, and evaluated hundreds of teachers. She has shown struggling teachers how to improve their teaching. She has worked with good teachers to help them become great teachers. She has guided great teachers whose goal was to pursue perfection. She has also disciplined defiant teachers, and she has convinced three teachers that they needed to change careers. Those three teachers knew they needed to change careers but needed the catalyst that Ruth provided.

Above all the lessons Ruth has learned about being a successful school principal, the most vital lesson is that the principal is not the most important position or person at the school. The quality of a school is determined by the effectiveness of the teachers, Ruth is convinced, more than it is determined by any other factor that educators can control. Ruth is devoted to students. The best way she can implement that devotion to students is by having the best possible teacher in every classroom providing students with the best possible learning experiences. Sounds good, but how is that done? Ruth says the answer has two parts and both parts are essential.

Ruth Matthews does not know Jonathan Bethel or Joe Peterson; however, Ruth has known many teachers whose thoughts about teaching are very similar to Jonathan's thoughts, and she has known many other teachers whose thoughts about teaching are very similar to Joe's thoughts. Ruth long ago concluded that the issue is not whether it is better to approach teaching with the perception of the idealistic dreamer or with the perception of the realistic jobber but rather to combine the dream and the reality into what she likes to call The TWIN approach. TWIN stands for Together Wisdom Is Nurtured.

Ruth is forever thankful to be the mother of her twin daughters, Julie and Katie. In appearance, Julie and Katie are truly identical twins. In personality, interests, ambition, and many other part of life, Julie and Katie are opposites, yet they are fully compatible. Julie and Katie have each made unique contributions to the family, and the family has benefitted from the unique contributions of each daughter. Julie loves to cook. Katie love to play piano. The Matthews family has enjoyed many evenings with a perfect meal that Julie prepared followed by a perfect piano concert that Katie presented. Details follow.

"IT TAKES TWO," BY RUTH MATTHEWS

One of the great joys and blessings in my life is being the mother of twin daughters. Perhaps it is then more accurate to say that two of the great joys of and blessings in my life is being the mother of two daughters.

As similar as my daughters are in appearance, they are just as different in personality, interest, ambition, and many other factors that express human uniqueness. The question has never been which daughter has a better personality, a better set of interests, or a better ambition; rather, the fact has always been that each daughter has a wonderful personality, many impressive interests, and highly honorable ambitions. Our family life is forever enriched by the fascinating and wholesome uniqueness of each daughter.

Teaching is similar. Throughout my years, make that decades, as an educator, I have worked with hundreds of teachers. For the most part, these teachers seemed to put themselves in one of two major categories. First are the teachers who are absolutely committed to doing whatever it takes to make every student completely successful. Some of those teachers get exhausted but are certain that, if they just work more hours each week, the desired results will arrive finally. Some of those teachers make a few adjustments and hold onto their dream but realize that progress is made with a series of small steps one person at a time rather than all at once with everyone.

Second are the teachers who are absolutely willing to do what their teaching contract requires and their job description includes. This group ranges from the conscientious to the lazy, but most of them complete their assigned tasks. They often do the same thing over and over, year after year, because that is what they were trained to do or is what they trained themselves to do. Some of those teachers do eventually make a few adjustments in what they do when they realize or are informed that the bell-shaped results in their classrooms are very predictable but that some or many of their students are doing better work and making better grades in other classes. The teachers in this group who complete their contractual obligations, fulfill the requirements of their job description, and then add creativity, variety, and humanity to their classroom can usually see improved learning results by their students and have better career results for themselves.

I have concluded that the most desired teaching combines the best of both approaches. It takes two together rather than either one alone to maximize results.

Schools need dreamers who fulfill all of their contractual obligations and all parts of their job description. Schools need workmanlike people who comply with their contract and their job description yet who realize that, while those documents are what is required, those documents should not be seen as a limit on how creatively, vibrantly, individually, or interpersonally the process of teaching and learning can be done.

Together wisdom is nurtured. A person does not become wise alone. A teacher does not become a wise teacher alone, perpetually into or onto himself or herself.

I have worked with the entire spectrum of teachers. I have worked with teachers who won awards for their superior work and with other teachers who were as good or better but never won an award. I never heard a complaint from those outstanding teachers who were overlooked by people who selected the award winners. For those teachers and for many others including some who actually win the awards, teaching effectively in ways that touch the lives of students is the award they seek and appreciate.

I have worked with some teachers who arrived at school early each morning and who stayed at school for extra hours after dismissal each day, who did extra work at school in the summer for no extra pay, who felt genuine anguish when any student failed, and who never paused to tell themselves that they had done wonderful work because they never reached perfection, because there was always something that could be better.

I try to advise these superachievers that it would be better to have a teaching career of thirty great years than to have a teaching career of perpetual frustration or, worse yet, to quit this profession because there could never be a time of perfection and there certainly could not be years of constant perfection. I do appreciate their dream of a perfect classroom. I do fear that they never realize how much good they are doing and how much their students are learning because their dream measures success as all or nothing, as perfection or failure. They could do themselves and their students some good if they adjusted their work standards from obsession to determined.

I have known many good teachers. In fact, that describes most of the teachers I have worked with. They saw teaching as more than a job but less than an emergency. They had an honorable commitment to their students; they were open to suggestions, ideas, new responsibilities, and constructive criticism. Some of them moved up to the great level in part of their work. Some of them moved to the ordinary level in some of their work. I always try to acknowledge the rise to greatness. I also try to elevate the work level whenever a good teacher—and there can be many reasons this happens temporarily—declines into the ordinary category.

Then I have known the teachers who barely do enough to avoid getting disciplined, reprimanded, put on probation, or fired. I do wonder why these people became teachers. They seem to get so little out of the experience of teaching. Of course, they put very little into their teaching. They have sometimes said to me, "What law am I breaking? Why policy did I violate? What is there in the contract that I am not living up to?"

One time, I gave this answer: If I am responsible for feeding you, I could give you three meals a day consisting of two slices of bread and one glass of water for each meal. I'm feeding you in terms of the contract, but am I giving you the real nutrition you need? Am I giving myself the satisfaction and the joy of knowing that I did my best for you?

Only a few of the teachers I have worked with were incapable of doing the job. Some of them were just stubborn or severely lazy. They refused to comply with very reasonable instructions about acceptable quality of work and acceptable quantity of work. Some of them quit. Some of them found a teaching job elsewhere. Some of them changed careers altogether. A few were fired or just were not hired for the next year. I recall one person who was told that he was not being rehired for the next year after he had endured two miserable years in the classroom. He said, "Finally. I never wanted to be a teacher. My family insisted. Now I can go work at my friend's car repair shop like I always wanted to."

My most memorable conversations, for very different reasons, with teachers are those discussions with the teachers who are so idealistic, so hopeful that they can be the teacher who makes everything right for everyone. Their idealism is inspiring, uplifting, and is needed.

The other group is the down-to-earth, by-the-book, by-the-contract, by-the-job-description teachers who are 100 percent consistent because they are 100 percent following the plans, procedures, and policies. Policies need to be obeyed; however, some policies need to be changed and are not worthy of permanence. Established procedures need to be followed; however, some procedures need to be improved, and people who never question a procedure or never think that a procedure can be improved, while providing stability, are also, in a way, limiting progress.

I have concluded that it takes two. A faculty of all dreamers would create a school of pursued, but unachieved, idealism. A faculty of down-to-earth realists would create a school of consistent, but never questioned or challenged, results. It takes both, but that does not mean having a faculty with 50 percent dreamers and 50 percent down-to-earth realists. Rather, it means that all teachers benefit from a blend of idealism and reality. Be a dreamer, but keep one foot, and sometimes both feet, on the ground.

What questions does the reader have for Ruth Matthews? Space is provided below:

1.

2.

3.

4.

5.

Together wisdom is nurtured. Ruth is advising us that wisdom calls for a blend of the dream of teaching and the reality of teaching, to create the most productive approach to teaching. Do you agree? Why? Do you disagree? Why?

The work of teaching requires heart, mind, body, and soul. The labor of teaching requires mind and body. What is it that heart and soul bring to teaching that elevates teaching from labor to work? By labor, we refer to the physical activity. By work, we refer to the meaning, purpose, commitment, and standards that can inspire greatness.

When a composer writes notes on a page, he or she is doing part of the labor of creating a symphony. When a composer creates a concept that the music is to convey, when the composer revises and revises to ensure that the music communicates the concept, and when the composer's music is understood by an orchestra and its conductor so a performance expresses much more than notes, it expresses emotion, interaction, ideas, and inspiration that impact the audience more than the notes themselves can; the music has become part of the works of the composer.

Jonathan Bethel understands teaching as his life's work. Joe Peterson understands teaching as his life's labor. Ruth Matthews would advise Jonathan and Joe to combine the best of work and labor into a liberating combination that enhances the classroom experience for students and for teachers.

Jonathan and other dreamers may get concerned whenever they take one step away from their dream toward accepting some of the realities of teaching. Dreamers may see that step as a compromise of their integrity.

Joe and other realists may get concerned whenever they take one step away from their reality toward accepting some of the dreamers' idealist hopes for teaching. Realists may see that as wasted time on one more social engineering experiment or on one more unproductive, trendy education fad.

How can these differing perspectives be blended into a more effective, more efficient, and more productive combination of dream and reality? One way is to check to see if all four resources are being applied—heart, mind, body, and soul. Dreamers tend to emphasize heart and soul. Realists tend to emphasize mind and body. The work of teaching requires heart, mind, body, and soul.

David Phillips will explain and will demonstrate how this is done. David has taught elementary school and middle school for a total of ten years. He currently teaches sixth-grade math and science classes.

I almost quit teaching at the end of the first semester of my first year. Nothing had gone right or, at least, it seemed that way to me. I was teaching math and science classes to fifth graders. Well, I was supposed to be doing that. I was young and naive and out to change the world. I was going to be the best friend those fifth graders ever had. I was going to get to know them and earn their trust, and after that we would learn so much. Well, that is how it was supposed to happen.

What did I do wrong? Everything. On the first day of school I told them that our class would be so much fun it would be like summer vacation never ended. To me, that meant we would do a lot of neat science experiments and some really creative math games. To them, that meant play.

I thought the fifth graders would do what I told them to do because, well, I was willing to do anything for them, so I figured they were old enough to appreciate someone like that and cooperate. I later learned I was far too optimistic.

I talked to an experienced teacher who told me I needed to set up a routine and a structure. She said that the fifth graders would interpret my friendliness as permission to do almost anything. I needed to be their teacher, not their big brother or their favorite uncle.

So, I set up a routine and a lot of structure. Every minute of each day was planned precisely. Nothing spontaneous could come up, interesting or not, educational or not, that would be allowed to divert us from the schedule, the routine, and the structure.

Apparently, I overcorrected. Going from commune to military school was a rocky ride for the students and for me. We struggled through October and November, but it really was not working for the students or for me. I talked to the principal in early December when we had our once-a-semester meeting for her to see how my first year of teaching was going. Principals in the school district were required to have a support plan for new teachers, and this meeting pretty much was the plan.

I wondered how direct I should be. Is it a good idea for a first-year teacher or any teacher to admit that things are bad and getting no better? I decided to be honest and explain that I had tried two completely different approaches and the record was zero wins, two losses. I asked for her advice. I almost expected her to suggest that I consider another line of work while I was still very young. She had a different idea.

"Mr. Phillips, twenty-one years ago, you were a fifth grader at this school. You said a lot about the wonderful experiences you had here as a student when we inter-viewed you. Have you considered doing for your students now what your teachers did for you back then? You know, some of those teachers are still on the faculty here. You pick a day very soon, and you spend that day going to observe your former teachers and other teachers. See your students in other classrooms. Find out what is working here. The assistant principal, the counselor, and I will each teach some of your classes for you that day. It will be good for us to be back in a classroom. Then you, the assistant principal, the counselor, and I will meet to dis-cuss what we experienced, what we learned, and what all of us think will work best in your classroom. We'll get this worked out. I'm sorry I was not aware of these situations earlier, but do not worry. We'll work together. We'll put our minds together on this, do a little soul searching, and get it all figured out."

It worked, not perfectly, but the second semester was so much better for the students and for me. I made some changes that began on the first day of the second semester. I continued to make adjustments based on what worked best. I listened to the students a lot more. I could not do everything they suggested, but I could implement some of their ideas. That seemed to help build a partnership in the classroom. Overall, the plan our principal set up helped a lot and was the major reason I was able to finish that school year with a real sense of achievement and with a determi-nation to continue being a teacher.

When I was in graduate school about seven years ago getting my master's degree, I wrote a paper about those first-year experiences. The professor told my class to write about this topic: "There Are Many Other Jobs and Many Other Careers, So Why Be a Teacher?" Here's my paper:

"THERE ARE MANY OTHER JOBS AND MANY OTHER CAREERS, SO WHY BE A TEACHER?" BY DAVID PHILLIPS

Is teaching a job? Do teachers go to work each day with the same attitude that bankers, mechanics, factory workers, and store managers take to their work? When teachers leave their home in the morning, do they say that it is time to go to work? Do teachers say that they have a job to do?

From the years I was a student in kindergarten through college, I have no memory of hearing a teacher or a professor refer to their job. Teachers and professors certainly have jobs in the sense of work to do for which they are paid. I had jobs during high school and college. Those jobs were done only to make money. Do teachers teach only to make money?

Many of my friends in college questioned my interest in teaching. "You'll never make any money" or "Why do you want to do that. Don't you want to get out of school instead of going right back into school?" My friends who were going to be lawyers, physicians, business managers, entrepreneurs, bankers, or scientists were eager to make large incomes doing a job that was interesting to them. I knew their income would be larger than mine, but my goal was not to be the wealthiest person at the thirtieth reunion of my college graduating class. My goal was to teach.

During my first semester of teaching, my goal was almost to change jobs immediately. My dream to be the best teacher my students ever had was colliding with the goal of many of my students to do nothing, learn nothing, frustrate me, and get in the way of the few students who were willing to obey, work, and learn. I was very serious about leaving the promised land of the classroom where originally I had planned to create the most amazing learning results known to mankind. I was ready for a job where a boss told me what to do, I did it, nobody disrupted or sabotaged my work, I got paid, and I could move up in the organization.

Then I found a way to make my teaching dream come true. The realization for me was that starting with the dream is a guarantee of failure, disappointment, and anguish. Start with reality and work toward the dream. Teach to the dream became my guideline rather than teach in the dream or dream about the dream. Teach, work, plan, create, revise, and the dream will follow. How did I learn all of this? Some wonderful people at the elementary school where I began my teaching career get the credit for taking me from almost quitting my teaching position to making a strong and more realistic commitment to teaching than I had originally brought to the classroom.

The principal, assistant principal, and school counselor selected a day, and they each taught one-third of my classes that day. I visited other classrooms to observe the very effective teaching methods and discipline methods other teachers were using.

I also observed my students in their other classes. I saw my students work hard and behave well in one class but do little work and misbehave in another class. It was the same group of students each time. The variables seemed to be what the teacher did and how the teacher did that.

I saw some classrooms that matched the dream, the ideal I had expected my classroom to be. That confirmed for me that it was not a fantasy to think that a teacher could work with students in ways that surpassed even the most ambitious goals.

I also saw some classrooms that needed help, just like my classroom did. I wondered then what could be done for more teachers to get the benefit of a school crisis response team effort similar to what the principal, assistant principal, and counselor were doing for me. During the past nine years of my career, I have worked with other teachers and the principal to organize internal improvement systems where teachers get many more opportunities to observe each other, observe their students, trade ideas about what works best, and find solutions for what is not working.

After the day during my first year of teaching, when those colleagues taught my fifth-grade classes for me, I met with the principal, assistant principal, and counselor along with two teachers whose classroom I observed. We agreed that all of them would visit my classroom occasionally to help me fine-tune my teaching methods and discipline system. We had a very productive meeting during which I took a lot of notes. The following summaries include the essential insights and words of wisdom that were shared with me.

The other teachers told me to emphasize instructional effectiveness. They told me to do what works with my students in my classes. They said not to copy or mimic what I observed them do but to borrow good ideas and then personalize them for the unique classroom community that my students and I create. Evidence for this was that those two great teachers did not use the exact same teaching methods. Also, they varied their teaching methods to apply and build upon the strengths of students and to address the needs of students in each separate class.

The teachers told me to emphasize academic learning. Fascinate the minds of students was one repeated statement. Fascinate the mind. What does that mean? What did those teachers expect me to do to fascinate the mind of each student? They explained that fifth graders have endless curiosities but that school can sometimes or most of the time see curiosity as inefficient. There are twenty-five math problems to complete, so there is no time to explain how a baseball player's batting average is calculated or what that statistic really means. The truth is, a project on sports statistics could make fifth-grade math so fascinating that doing the twenty-five related math problems is worth it more than ever.

The assistant principal told me to take good care of my health. She also told me to avoid designing the instructional plan for any class period where the students had to sit in their chair or at their desk for the entire class.

My body has to be healthy or the work I would like to do with my students will suffer. I am rarely absent from school—only eight days missed in ten years of teaching—so I will do almost anything to avoid being absent. The best way to avoid absences is to be healthy. For me, that means not to work eighty hours per week. I have become convinced that I accomplish more with sixty-five to seventy hours of great work than with seventy to eighty hours of good yet weary work. Those ten hours I do not work now, which I might have been inclined to work before, I can now use to get lots of exercise. A great teacher needs a healthy body.

I design a two-minute physical activity into each class period or into each hour, depending on whether students are with me less than or more than an hour. The students might divide into groups and then we combine two groups to see what new fraction was created. Thirty students divided into three groups of five students plus five groups of three students could combine into multiple groups that create many new fractions. Children seem to think better when they can move around and see how a concept, an idea, or a problem can be analyzed, explored, and figured out.

The counselors asked me an unexpected question: how would you describe the soul of your classroom? My first reply was "describe the what," and they said, "the soul, you know, the spirit, the energy, the personality, the vitality of your classroom, which is there only when you and your students are in a classroom world of you own."

I told them I did not know the answer because I had never been told that my classroom should have a soul. They were ready for my lack of an answer. They handed me an empty balloon. They told me to describe it. Then they told me to fill it with air. Then I was to describe the inflated balloon. Then I was told to let the air out and then blow it up again. I finally got the point. My classroom is the balloon with no air until the students and I breathe into the room life, energy, ideas, personalities, imagination, work, trust, rules, discoveries, challenges, improvements, mistakes made and corrected, discipline, and commitment. Those ingredients help put a soul into a classroom.

The principal had very important advice about classroom-management techniques, about classroom discipline methods, about effective teaching methods, about pacing myself to avoid exhaustion, about use of a variety of instructional activities, about how to keep up with the increased amount of paperwork or computer record keeping, and about communication with parents or guardians.

Then the principal asked me a question that was similar to what the counselors had asked: "So, Mr. Phillips, are you putting your heart into your teaching?" My limited reply was "Am I doing what?" The principal tried again. "Mr. Phillips, with the work you are doing in your classroom for and with your students, would it be obvious to your students and to any visitor that you are not just doing the actions of a teacher but that your dedication to teaching comes from your heart. You know, Mr. Phillips, when you teach, is it obvious that you are enthusiastic about students and learning and teaching and school? Is it obvious that you sincerely love being a teacher?"

Many thoughts raced through my mind. Did my teaching contract say that I had to love teaching? Does the principal's contract say she has to love being a principal? If I loved teaching, would I be thinking of changing careers? If I did not love teaching, or at least like teaching and be willing to try and like it more, would I be seeking advice from the principal and these other colleagues? Finally, I realized what my answer honestly was. "I love teaching part of the time, but those parts are less than I expected. I would prefer to love teaching than wrestle with teaching like I've been doing. So, yes, I want to love teaching, and it would help if teaching loved me back."

The principal told me that was an answer she could work with. She explained that, if I could dig down deeply and put my heart into this work even when it was disappointing, frustrating, annoying, or exhausting, then teaching would love me back. Why? Because teaching would respond to my unlimited resilience. As I learned more from colleagues, from experience, from teaching, from reading, from my own thinking, I would increasingly realize that the bond I can have with teaching is truly from my heart to the heart of teaching. I would dismiss such lofty thoughts as far too idealistic were they not based on a solid foundation of work and knowledge.

So, why be a teacher? Because more than any other job, work, career, or position that exists, teaching and I need each other. Teaching is part of who I am, but teaching very well is a bigger part of who I can become. As I become a better teacher, teaching provides better experiences for my students, and the teaching profession gains new knowledge about itself from me. This is where I belong. This is who I am. That's why I am a teacher.

Mr. Phillips had the opportunity during his first year of teaching to think anew about the work of a teacher and whether that work was the best investment of his career years. He renewed his dedication to teaching after some serious analysis, thinking, advice, creative professional development, and sincere soul searching. Mr. Phillips found many more reasons and many stronger reasons to teach than he found quantity or quality of reasons not to teach. Mr. Phillips signed a very demanding yet very rewarding and meaningful contract with himself to properly and reasonably apply his heart, mind, body, and soul to teaching.

Another person finding themselves in the same job circumstances and workplace realities as Mr. Phillips in the first year of teaching might decide to finish that year and never return. For that person, teaching's demands are too many and rewards are too few. For that person, the reality of teaching overpowers any dream of teaching. Perhaps, for that person, there is just a realization that what they expected teaching to be and what teaching is now or could become are eventually so far apart that there will never be any genuine compatibility between that person and teaching.

The decisions will vary from person to person when the most difficult realities of teaching are confronted. Is it worth the effort to endure? Is it time to work elsewhere? Can I reasonably apply my heart, mind, body, and soul to teaching? Is there another career to which I can more deeply, more productively, and more symbiotically apply my heart, mind, body, and soul? Is there another career that will not require so much of my heart, mind, body, and soul? Is there a career that requires less than all four of those parts of a human at work? Would such careers be a better match for me?

Mr. Phillips realized that the work that matters most to him is to teach students. That realization means he had to be where students are—in classrooms at school. Mr. Phillips also realized that to fully achieve his dream of teaching he had to fully encounter, deal with, and master the reality of teaching. By applying his heart, mind, body, and soul to teaching, David Phillips could be true to his teaching dream while dealing directly with teaching's realities.

Now that the reasons to be a teacher and the reasons not to be a teacher have been explored, and now that the truth that the work of teaching requires heart, mind, body, and soul has been confirmed, our attention turns to another dimension of the dream and the reality of teaching: teaching is not what you expect.

Chapter Three

Teaching Is Not What You Expect

To a student in elementary school, middle school, or high school, it may appear that teachers work thirty-five hours per week. The school day is seven hours long, and school is in session five days per week, so the conclusion for any student who thinks about the topic could be that teachers work thirty-five hours each week.

How did the tests this student takes get typed, copied, graded, and the grades recorded in a written grade book and in the computer? The teacher did all of that.

How did the activities done in each class get organized and planned? How did the page about the next homework project get written, typed, copied, and handed out? Who will grade those projects? The teacher does all of that.

How did that list of Internet websites for students to use on a research project get compiled? How did these great-looking and very informative posters get into this classroom and onto the walls? How did these really interesting guest speakers end up coming to our classroom? How did our tests get graded so fast and with individualized comments telling each student what was good about his or her writing and what needed to improve in the writing? The teacher did all of that.

How did a parent know about the great question his son asked in class? How did another parent know that her daughter is making B and C grades instead of the A grades she made earlier in the year? How did the principal know to come to a certain class and congratulate the students for the outstanding work they did on a recent class project? The teacher made all of that happen. All of that was in addition to the thirty-five hours per week of classroom instruction during school days. The total hours in a week for a conscientious teacher can easily reach sixty-five to seventy. For some very highly motivated and very willing-to-do-whatever-is-needed teachers—including overachievers, perfectionists, or extreme dreamers—the total of work hours per week can reach seventy-five or eighty. That work schedule may not be what people expected when they prepared for or when they began their teaching career.

The realities of teaching cannot be and should not be denied, but they can be and should be dealt with. The truth that these realities exist need not be the only factor that determines the work a teacher can do or must do. The first step in being prepared for reality is to identify reality. This is a long journey, because the reality of teaching is complex, but that reality must be known, understood, and confronted to succeed in teaching. The topics that follow are some of the many parts within the overall reality of teaching, but the reader will think of additional parts. This long, yet incomplete list, confirms how vast, complex, challenging, and identifiable the reality of teaching is. Knowing these realities is step 1. Knowing how to respond to these realities is step 2. Remembering that a teacher can control how he or she confronts these realities is what creates an advantage for the tenacious teacher whose dream will not be denied because current realities are genuine, but need not be permanent or need not be decisive. "A new reality can be created" is the optimist's perception. "The current reality offers resistance to any effort," replies the pessimist. The bold yet practical approach searches for ways to react to these realities of teaching and make those reactions support the dream of teaching.

1. Morning hallway duty and other similar duties:

It is possible and it may be common that teachers will be given nonteaching tasks that come under the contractual responsibility to accept "other duties as assigned." An example is morning hallway duty, which is intended to place some teachers throughout the school building during part of the time between when students have arrived at school and the instructional day begins. Whether students are given any or many choices about how this early time can be used will vary from school to school and will also vary from elementary school to middle school to high school.

When a person interviews for a teaching job, it is most unlikely for questions to be asked about how you will do your morning hallway duty when it is your turn. What possible answer could be given other than to affirm that you certainly will accept your part of the work for the good of the school?

There are two major realities about morning hallway duty. First, even though your highest priority is to be an effective teacher, even though you would rather use this early morning half hour to grade papers or prepare lessons, and even though the fact of morning hallway duty was never mentioned during your college years in any teacher preparation class you took, duties such as this are part of the reality of the teaching job.

Second, there are different ways to experience morning hallway duty. You could try to grade papers, but the papers would get part of your attention and the students in the hallways would get part of your attention. Your divided attention means the papers are not graded well and the halls are not supervised well.

You could accept this duty as an opportunity to talk with students rather than resent this duty as an unfair chore. As you see students whom you teach or have taught, you could have a pleasant visit with them asking about how school is going for them and seeing if they have everything ready for the day at school.

Morning hallway duty and its cousins—morning or afternoon bus area duty, athletic game duty, and homeroom supervision—are within the reality of the teaching job. A teacher can angrily resent these interferences with the real work of teaching, or a teacher can positively make these parts of the real work of teaching. Teachers will not be able to make these duties go away. Teachers are able to make the most of these duties. These duties are parts of the teaching reality, but if done with some energy and imagination, these duties also can support the teaching dream.

2. Paperwork:

The paperwork never ends. A paperless classroom that uses electronic screens for everything that paper used to do is an electronic form of paperwork.

Do interview questions for a teaching position include "What is your philosophy of education, what is your classroom-management system, and how do you keep up with large amounts of paperwork?" Questions 1 and 2 are common. Has question 3 ever been asked? Yet question 3 deals with one very realistic part of teaching, and despite the assumption that people will figure out how to keep up with all of the paperwork, doing the paperwork efficiently enhances a teacher's classroom results.

Consider a high school English teacher who has five classes and a total of 140 students. The English department at the school has agreed that every student in each English class will write at least one paper per week. The English department has also agreed that papers will be returned to students within two days so the comments from the teacher can be read by the students while the paper that was written is still a fresh memory for the students.

One English teacher decides that her first-period class will turn in its weekly writing on Monday, her second-period class will turn in its weekly paper on Tuesday, and that this sequence will continue through the week so each day there is one set of papers turned in—twenty-eight papers times five minutes per paper to grade equals 140 minutes of grading those papers each day. There will be other paperwork to do, lessons to plan, tests to grade, special projects to grade, reading assignments to discuss in class, and grades to record in the paper grade book and in the computer.

Is there more? Yes. The teachers are required to maintain a log of all communication with families of students; there are forms to fill out to attend a professional development program; lesson plans have to be copied and given to an assistant principal; discipline referrals are written as needed; documentation of all discipline action that did not require a formal discipline referral must be maintained and made available as needed for meetings about a student; surveys are sent to teachers for completion; attendance is taken each class period; and emergency materials for a substitute teacher must be updated and must be easily available for a day when the teacher is absent and had no way to anticipate the absence.

The paperwork demands of teaching surpass the common expectation. Can the paperwork be reduced? Some of it can be changed from paperwork to the computer version of the same task, but the time involved may be similar. "I can't wait to be a teacher so I can grade papers for twenty to thirty hours each week and do lots of other paperwork" is not what future teachers are thinking as they prepare for their career, but the paperwork is part of the reality of teaching.

Consider this question: how can the paperwork be done in ways that support the dream of teaching? The detailed and individualized comment a teacher takes three minutes to write on a student's paper could result in significantly better work by and behavior by that student. Please think of other ways that relate to what paperwork is done or how the paperwork is done that could make the reality of paperwork support the dream of teaching and list your ideas:

1.

2.

3.

4.

5.

3. Computer work:

E-mail and other versions of instant electronic communication eliminate the inefficient, unproductive, frustrating sequence of telephone tag where call after call resulted in message after message, but no direct communication or interaction.

E-mail helpfully removed the time and place limitations of the telephone, voice mail notwithstanding. Two people do not need to be on the phone at the same time to communicate, thanks to the liberating flexibility of e-mail. That sounds good, but are there any problems with this new communication freedom? Yes.

When a phone call was made, it was person A talking with person B. With e-mail, person A sends the message to the one person or to more people who then reply or forward the message to more people. The phone call was finite. E-mail can be infinite. More communication is not always better communication. New communication methods do not ensure quality communication content.

E-mail, computers in general, and other electronic creations provide teachers with some very beneficial options. For people who began teaching prior to the personal computer and Internet revolutions, old habits have had to encounter endless innovations. For people who began teaching after those technology revolutions, there are the simplicities of not having to learn anew how the latest method of showing a one-minute video clip through the computer and the projector has brought that process many steps beyond the old filmstrips, slide presentations, or reel-to-reel movies.

For a twenty-two-year-old who recently graduated from college and who is entering the first year of teaching, the aspect of teaching that may not equal what was expected could be that the use of technology at the college campus was more advanced and was almost ubiquitous compared to the new teacher's eighth-grade classroom. For the forty-four-year-old teacher with twenty-two years of traditional teaching experience, the aspect of teaching today that may not equal what was expected could be that the use of technology expands and increases annually while raising new questions about the best ways to teach. The technology debate can include topics such as the use of technology because the machines are available; use of technology because an investment was made to show everyone how to use the newest technological advances; use of technology when it selectively is the best way to cause the intended learning; or use of technology because a grant requires that use.

Some professional development programs can be taken by teachers online. That could be efficient, yet the online version of useless professional development is still useless. A teacher's Web page can provide helpful information to students and their parents or guardians. Teachers can design productive research activities for students to complete using the Internet, yet designing academic assignments that are Internet proof—meaning the Internet cannot do all of the work for the student—is a new challenge for teachers.

Because surveys are easily designed for online use, does this option create more surveys, some of which are meaningful while others merely fill some bureaucratic process? That process can be aided by the potential reality that work expands to fill the capability of the computer rather than the real need for information.

The use of technology in education has increased and will increase. This creates new debates and new opportunities. The same Internet that enables a student to quickly locate a vital document for U.S. history class also tempts some students to find a website with analysis of that document. Will the student read and think about the quickly accessed document, or will the student cut and paste some Internet paragraphs and turn those in for the required homework analysis? That question and the yet-to-be-created new versions of that question are parts of the technology aspect of teaching being different from what was expected.

It is five in the morning, and snow has caused school to be cancelled for the day. A teacher goes to her computer at home and in twenty minutes updates the snow day assignments for her students to complete. The weather problem will not create an instructional problem. This and many other innovative possibilities of technology are part of what was not expected within teaching some years ago but are part of what technology can help a teacher offer to exceed a past year's limits.

4. Public address system interruptions:

They happen. The number of times they happen will vary from school to school. There will be a moment when a teacher and a class are one idea away from complete mastery of a complicated concept, the perfectly designed lesson has worked precisely, all students are attentive and are thinking, and then . . .

> Pardon this interruption, but the bus is here to take students to the conference at the university. Those students going to the conference should move to the bus loading area now. We apologize that there was no advance notice, but this opportunity for twelve students just came up yesterday. The names of the students were e-mailed to teachers a few minutes ago after all approvals were arranged.

Two of your students are leaving class now to go to the bus. You have to check your e-mail to confirm that they are on the list. The classroom instruction will continue, but the interruption is an academic injury. The perfect moment for maximum learning that the teacher and the students had worked conscientiously to create cannot be duplicated; rather, it will have lost its one unique chance to be everything the teacher hoped for. The instruction after the public address (PA) system interruption completes the lesson functionally but without the fascination that the learning crescendo would have created had the intellectual momentum not been interrupted.

Is this something that just has to be endured? Can this be minimized or prevented?

5. Meetings:

Some meetings at schools occur because it has been one week since the last meeting. Some groups meet weekly or monthly or on another regular schedule because it has always been done that way. Some groups meet to take serious action about serious topics. Some groups meet, meet, and keep meeting as a way to delay or to avoid taking any action. Every teacher will have meetings to attend, some of which will be productive while others will be a waste of time. There are probably more meetings that teachers attend than they expected would be the case when they prepared to become teachers or when they began teaching. What explains all of these meetings? Are they necessary? Do they improve academic results in classrooms? Are they merely the reality of being part of a large organization with some or with many bureaucratic characteristics?

Meetings that involve teachers include, but are not limited to, the following: faculty meetings, grade-level meetings, subject/department meetings, special education meetings, conferences with a parent or guardian about a student, meetings with school counselors, meetings to prepare for annual required tests, open house evenings at school, meetings to discuss new policy proposals, meetings for everyone to be informed about and trained in new procedures, and others the reader can add to the list.

1.

2.

3.

4.

5.

"I never expected there would be so many meetings. Some of this could be done with e-mails." "I never expected there would be so many e-mails telling us to do something. Maybe some of this needs to be done in a meeting so we can ask questions together and reach some agreement together."

It is reality that meetings will occur. The challenges are to make the meetings productive, efficient, and supportive of the most important work at school: teaching to cause learning.

6. *Lesson plans:*

> I was taught in college an exact system for developing a lesson plan. One college class required us to create a semester worth of lesson plans for a class we would teach. It took forever to do, but my plans were great. Then I get to my first teaching job and the school has a completely different form that teachers have to use, plus lesson plans for the next week are due to the assistant principal by 8:00 a.m. each Friday in paper form or electronically. I'm starting to think that the assistant principal never reads these. It's just one more checklist to be sure that some teacher who would never plan anything will have to put something on paper.

> I hear some teachers say they just use the lesson summaries that textbook publishers provide. I really never expected to hear that. I was taught in college all the intricate steps of instructional design. A serious teacher meticulously designs instruction based on what she knows about her students and based on what the students need to learn. How can people just turn in that ordinary, plain vanilla stuff that comes free with textbooks?

> The best lesson plans have to be changed. What we prepare for classes might work as planned, but usually you have to make some changes as you go. Why put all those hours into planning lessons if things are just going to change. Then there are the absent students or the students who sleep in class or the students who never pay attention no matter what lesson you plan. We usually just go page to page in the book. It works and no time gets wasted.

> This happens every few years. Somebody at the state department of education gets some regulation imposed on us about lesson plans or the school board members hear some presentation at a conference about the ultimate process for lesson plans. Just go along with it. Fill out the forms each week. These trends come and go, so this one will go pretty soon. You can expect some fad like this every few years.

Lesson plan disputes, fads, controversies, trends, deadlines, and formats can consume more time than future teachers expect and can consume more time than current teachers would prefer. Planning of high-quality lessons is essential. The format or paperwork associated with those high-quality lessons should not become the larger issue. High-quality lessons, planned well and implemented well, matter more than lesson plan trends or formats. Still, expect some lesson plan disputes, fads, controversies, trends, and related issues or nonissues to arise occasionally. Great lessons designed and implemented well support the dream of teaching. Trivial and bureaucratic lesson plan procedures are within the reality of teaching. The latter should not control or lessen the former.

7. Makeup work:

Students will be in class, students will be on time for class, students will turn in homework on time, students will realize how important tests are so they will let nothing keep them from class on test days, and students will realize that makeup work is an inconvenience for the teacher. How many of those statements do you expect will match the reality of teaching? How many of those statements would experienced teachers say match their reality?

School districts and individual teachers have policies about makeup work. Follow the policy you are given or establish your policy and follow it. Make-up work is extra work for teachers. Students will be absent occasionally and can turn in work when they return according to the policy. Makeup work is going to be with teachers forever. Can technology help? Can incentives for better school attendance by students help?

The reality of makeup work is not a reason to select a different career or to leave teaching after a few years. Makeup work is a reality. Create a schedule and a system to manage it. What ideas do you have to help makeup work be less of an inconvenience and more of a learning experience?

8. Defiance:

- "I don't do homework."
- "I never take a book home."
- "I never study for tests."
- "I usually copy somebody else's homework."
- "There's no way I am going to give you my phone. It's not my fault it rang in class."
- "I'm not cleaning that mess up. She caused it. Make her clean it up."
- "Just because you're the teacher does not make you in charge of me."
- "I heard you tell us to read. I don't feel like reading."
- "Just write a referral on me. I'm not moving to the desk you told me to move to."
- "I'm not taking the test. I don't care about my grade. This school stuff is stupid. It's easier to drop out and get a job."

College students decided to go to college. There is no compulsory attendance law for college that applies to students who have graduated from high school or who are over a certain age. The fact that college students are in school by choice implies a certain level of commitment to and appreciation of the academic work that colleges and universities require. The defiant college student who refuses to do any academic work will flunk out of college.

The elementary school, middle school, or high school student who occasionally or often is defiant is disciplined, counseled, met with, and usually given additional opportunities to do what is right and responsible. Few college students who are intentionally working toward teacher certification and college graduation are in the habit of defiance; rather, they are expected to comply with college requirements and they expect that of themselves. Some younger students live a defiant lifestyle. Are college students whose career will be teaching told to anticipate defiance from their future students? Do current teachers see defiance as another part of the school reality, or do they see eliminating, or at least reducing, defiance as part of the dream?

Are any adults who work at school ever defiant or, in stronger policy language, insubordinate? Not if they intend to have some workplace harmony with their employer and not if they intend to have a long career in education. Honest disagreements and lively debates in search of school improvements can be productive. Unfounded criticism, refusal to follow policies, and chronic complaints despite reasonable actions taken to address concerns are counterproductive or worse.

9. Colleagues who complain constantly:

- "My classroom is so cold. The air conditioning never works right."
- "My classroom is so hot. The furnace is always either too hot or not hot enough."
- "Can you believe that the copy machines are broken again?"
- "Another faculty meeting. The administrators are just going to do what they want to anyway. Why do they pretend to listen to us?"
- "Can you believe that a student is missing the first week of school for a family vacation? They had all summer, but no, they have to be out of town right when school starts. And somebody at the central office told them it would be excused absences."
- "Another fire drill. We just had one. And we just had the earthquake drill. When do we get to have a day of school without this other stuff?"
- "Can you believe the e-mail about putting grades in the computer no later than one week after the work was turned in? Who can get papers done that fast all the time?"
- "My substitute teacher from yesterday left notes that the students did nothing. She left another note saying the lesson plan was inadequate. Come on. I told her to have them read chapter 9 and answer the questions at the end of the chapter. What more does she want?"
- "How can the counselors and the administrators expect me to get a student through a year of high school English when she is absent more than she is here? They told me to give her the makeup work for the first semester. That's like teaching another class. Will I get paid to teach another class?"

Some topics, issues, decisions, actions, or inactions at schools merit criticism and correction. Other topics, issues, decisions, actions, or inactions really could reflect the best that is available now. Some people understand the difference and use their voices, suggestions, and criticism to improve schools. Other people seem to live to criticize. These constant critics can pollute the workplace atmosphere of a school, especially when their constant criticism is not matched with constant action to teach well and to improve the school.

The reality is that some people at school complain often. It is rarely useful to join their chorus of criticism, but when criticism is valid and action can be reasonably taken to improve something at school, that approach can support the dream.

Are future teachers told to beware of the constant critics? Are current teachers aware of how destructive any implied or actual encouragement of the constant critics can be?

10. Wonderful people to work with:

- "Let me know if there is anything I can help you with."
- "We used this newspaper article in class today. I made some extra copies for you. It might be something you could use."
- "Sure, I can do your early morning duty for you tomorrow so you can attend that parent meeting about your student."
- "I can show you how that works. All of us are getting used to this new computer program for entering grades. I did some work on it this summer, so I'll show you what I know."
- "I heard you talking about needing more resources about World War II. One of our teachers has an amazing collection of World War II papers and medals that her father received when he fought in that war. Come on, I'll introduce you, and she'll be glad to let you use those things."
- "Those forms are hard to figure out. One of the secretaries in the office is the expert. I'll tell you what I know about the forms and then we'll walk to her office."
- "It is frustrating when you work so hard on preparing for class and then some other teacher's field trip takes five or six of your students away. Maybe we need some policy about giving everyone enough notice before a field trip."

When students are asked about the best teacher they ever had, usually the student describes an extraordinarily caring, challenging, enthusiastic, and creative teacher who was always willing to go an extra mile for students. Such teachers are still in schools today and are willing to go the extra mile for students or for colleagues. There are equally caring and capable staff members at school whom principals may describe as "the person who really runs this place." New teachers and experienced teachers benefit from building strong, sincere bonds with these school angels. They can help you navigate the reality of teaching. They can also help you pursue your dream for teaching.

11. Students who write a note thanking you:

- "Because of your class I am prepared for college and for life."
- "You were always there for me, especially when things were so tough for me. I don't know what would have happened to me without your help."
- "You showed me how to read. Other teachers tried, but it never worked. You knew what I needed. Thank you for caring so much about me."
- "I worked harder in your class than in any class I ever had. I never knew I could work so hard. You made it interesting to learn. Now I know what I am capable of."
- "I never had a teacher who loves to teach as much as you do. Your excitement got everyone in our class excited. Thanks for an experience I'll remember forever."
- "When I made an F on our first test, you showed me exactly what I did wrong and how to fix it. In other classes, when I made an F, it was just an F. You showed me that I was better than F grades. When I made a B on our semester exam it changed my entire attitude about school."

No teacher is certain to hear a student express the thoughts in the above paragraphs. Teachers may hope, pray, work, and dream to have such an impact; however, actually hearing from a student that the student realized the impact, appreciates the impact, and is going to build upon the benefits of the impact surpass what can be expected.

There are moments when teaching is better than can be expected, when teaching is more rewarding than can be expected, and when teaching is more meaningful than can be expected. Those moments confirm that the dream of teaching can be experienced. Those moments confirm that the realities of teaching are worth enduring when they are difficult and are to be embraced when they are mastered as a foundation for the intended results.

Some of the realities of teaching are joyous. Some of the realities of teaching are painful. Reality has joy and pain. Embrace the one and confront the other.

12. The extra work you do that is never acknowledged:

You arrive early so a student can make up a test, so a parent can meet with you, so grades can be entered into the computer before papers are returned to students, so copies can be made of an activity you created for your students, so you can select and preview a two-minute video for use in class today, so you can complete all preparations for a debate students will have in a class today, and so your academic preparation for today is completed before you go to your early morning supervision duty in the cafeteria.

You stay late after school so a student can make up your physics test after she makes up her calculus test. You stay after school to check on materials in the library that your classes will use tomorrow. You stay later after school to make copies of upcoming tests; to attend two meetings; to meet with a counselor about helping a student get a highly competitive scholarship; to clean the surfaces of each desk in your classroom in hopes of fighting the flu outbreak; to type a quiz for one class and details of a homework project for another class; to select and check ten websites that students will access for a carefully designed research activity that a class will do in the computer lab next week; to grade one set of quiz papers plus put those grades in the computer and in the written grade book; to watch part of a soccer game because several of your students are on the school's team; and to write three letters of recommendation for three students to use with their college applications.

You grade papers for two to three hours or prepare lessons for two to three hours per night at home. You grade long writing assignments and tests during a weekend, realizing by Sunday night that the grading work required thirteen hours. You come to school to work five times in June, six times in July, and three times in early August to complete some analysis of last year's results and to prepare everything for the first week of the upcoming school year. You read and study each day during the summer because that makes you a better teacher.

Expect no acknowledgment of this extra work. Your motive for doing this extra work is not because someone else will notice. Your motives include your understanding of what teaching is and what teaching can be. Your motives include the work standard you set for yourself that surpasses any standard your employer could set. Your motives include your work ethic and your conscience, which insist that what can be done must be done.

There might be a rare occasion when you hear someone at school say, "You sure are staying late tonight." There might be another rare occasion when a quick verbal "thank-you" is stated by someone you are doing extra work for. Those occasions will never equal the sense of peace that comes from knowing that, despite the difficulties of the reality that teaching is, you did everything possible to elevate that reality toward the dream of teaching, which, also on wonderful occasions, does come true.

13. Your perfect attendance that is never acknowledged:

You come to school every day because you require that of yourself. The morning you wake up feeling about 75 percent healthy inspires you to heal yourself, energize yourself, and persist. Of course, illness that could spread to other people and illness that could be serious should get thorough attention and may force an absence. On the days when some people might call for a substitute teacher because they feel a bit weary, they just need a day off, or it is a sunny Friday in April are days you resist any temptation to miss school because then you would deny yourself the satisfaction of doing your work well.

Teachers may expect their colleagues to make every effort to be at school. Most teachers will live up to that attendance standard and expectation; however, there will be teachers who miss school up to the maximum number of sick days and personal days, and then never miss a day because that would mean a day without pay. Emergencies do occur, but emergencies do not occur on three consecutive Fridays during the peak beauty of autumn or spring. Expect to be frustrated that your perfect attendance is not acknowledged and that some people abuse the sick day process. You expect yourself to be at school every day if at all possible. That is your standard. That is your reality because making the dream of teaching happen requires being at school.

14. Students who have given up on school:

"Give up" does not mean a student does enough to make the lowest possible D grade in each class. "Give up" does not mean a student turns in work sometimes. "Give up" does not mean attend school most days. "Give up" means a student has decided that no schoolwork is worth the time or effort. "Give up" means to actually drop out of school or to remain enrolled but to have dropped out virtually as measured by doing no work and often or usually being absent. "Give up" means that, if a court deals with the student's truancy, the student might follow the least plan of action to satisfy the court, or it might mean that the student ignores the court to see if the justice system really will take action.

New teachers, experienced teachers, and college students preparing for a teaching career have some level—low, medium, or high—of excitement about school. That excitement can encounter a classroom shock when the eager teacher is face to face with a student who has given up on school completely or with students who have given up on school. Such a student, on the days he or she comes to school, goes to the cafeteria to eat breakfast and then avoids work until lunch when it is time to eat and socialize. The student then skips classes or disrupts classes until it is time to get on a bus and go home.

Ask other teachers who teach or who have taught this student for their advice about what could work. Ask the counselors and administrators for their guidance and involvement. Contact the student's parent or guardian. If a social worker or court official is involved, seek their help. Keep records of all efforts you make.

Now, look at the other 98- percent or 99 percent of your students who have not given up on school. Give them an equal amount of effort per student as you invest in the student who gave up on school. The problems of school are not the parts of teaching that define the whole. The reality of problems does not deny the possibility of making progress toward the dream.

15. Time demands:

Your family, friends, health, volunteer work, religious activities, hobbies, church league softball team, chores at home, errands to run, car needing to be serviced, and social events, in addition to the unexpected events that can occur at any moment and demand your time, do not relate to teaching duties, but the same person who has teaching duties also has personal duties such as those listed above. Will twenty-four hours per day be sufficient time to honor all of the demands on your time?

At school, the principal could tell the teachers that the national, state, and local authorities in education are mandating that every school take additional action to reduce the achievement gap between demographic groups of students, to be sure that every student reads at grade level, and to increase the high school graduation rate by 50 percent in four years. That graduation rate improvement, for example, would take a school's graduation rate from 90 percent to 95 percent or from 86 percent to 93 percent, reducing the difference between the current rate and 100 percent by 50 percent.

In addition to the extra work involved with those new goals and their resulting new initiatives, programs, meetings, and paperwork, teachers will continue to have lessons to plan, papers to grade, other meetings to attend, copies to make, makeup work to supervise, grades to enter in the grade book and in the computer, professional development programs to attend, and much more.

All of this must get done. How? Learn the proven methods of time management. Get in the habit of saying no. The elementary school bake sale organizing committee will get their work done without you. The papers you need to grade will not get graded without you. The middle school dance or the high school homecoming parade are events a teacher could enjoy supervising, but is that supervision the best use of your time on that day? If yes, grade the papers the day before. If no, tell the person who asks you to supervise that your schedule for family duties and teaching activities require you to say no.

The time realities of teaching have some surprises. The lesson you spent one hour preparing and that you thought would fill a class period is completed by all students in twelve minutes. Now what? The essay question you added to the multiple-choice question test was a very well-worded question that sparked profound ideas from your students. A machine grades the multiple-choice part of the test in two minutes. You grade the essay question part in four hours. Students must write to improve their writing skills and their analytical skills. One reality of their skill improvement is four hours of a teacher's time to thoroughly grade and comment on the papers. Someone who does not have essays to grade that day can help supervise the dance or the parade.

The reality of time in teaching is that doing the work of a great person, a great family member, and a great teacher means each day's time is 100 percent obligated. Time must be managed. "No" must be said. The time reality must be mastered so the dream is not absorbed in a vortex of too much to do and too little time in which to do it.

16. School working conditions versus other workplaces:

Every workplace—schools, retail businesses, government offices, hospitals, factories, medical offices, and others—have conditions the employees like and other conditions the employees dislike. There is no perfect place to work.

The minute-to-minute, hour-to-hour, day-to-day, and year-to-year working condition realities at schools are some of the factors that help create the atmosphere of the arena in which the dreams of a teacher must somehow thrive. What are some of those school working conditions?

Teachers do their own typing. Teachers make the copies of any materials they will distribute to students. Teachers grade tests, homework, projects, and other assignments. The classroom work of a teacher can be interrupted at any time with no warning and with no limit when situations such as these occur: an administrator has to see a certain student *now*; the school office manager calls a classroom to find a student; another teacher calls the classroom thinking his or her desire to find a student is more important than your need to teach that same student; and a family member comes to school to take a student to an appointment that could have been scheduled for after school, but the student plays a sport and would never miss athletic practice, plus the parent is hoping for an athletic scholarship so she permits the student to miss class but not athletics.

When does a teacher go to the bathroom? Leaving the classroom unattended is unacceptable. The hours between when the school day begins and lunch can create some unhealthy delays. What's a teacher to do?

Teachers eat lunch when their students eat lunch. The time allotted is probably close to thirty minutes. Teachers might bring their lunch or go to the school cafeteria. During those thirty minutes, a teacher may have phone calls to make or to return, copies to make for afternoon classes because in the time before classes began this morning the copy machines were not working, and e-mails to check.

Teachers may work in a building that was awarded to the lowest bidder for construction. This same building has supplies that are from the lowest bidder, whether the item in question is desks for students or computers for teachers. The lowest-bid approach is designed to save money, yet if it creates a working condition where continuous repairs are needed, it is not necessarily saving money and it is negatively impacting the work environment.

Teachers rarely have a career path. There is usually not a formal career sequence of apprentice teacher, permanently certified teacher, advanced teacher, distinguished teacher, and master teacher. The best teachers create their personal career path by doing what is needed to improve their teaching skills and results each year. Their improvement is rarely officially acknowledged by their profession. The typical career advancement merit option for teachers is to leave the classroom and enter an aspect of school administration. There are ample challenges and experiences within a classroom to fill a career with abundant opportunities to grow professionally every year of a long teaching career. The profession will not officially acknowledge that growth, but good teachers who work to become great teachers and then to become exemplary teachers can occasionally acknowledge to themselves that they have boldly mastered the realities of teaching so they could magnificently live their dreams for teaching.

17. You learn with and from students:

"I think that if Mondale had won the 1984 presidential election we would have stopped the deficits and avoided the money problems we are in now." That is a profound thesis. When a student makes that kind of statement in a U.S. history class, the teacher could encourage him to write a book to fully develop his insight. The student stretches the mind, thinking, and perception of the teacher. The student instructs everyone in the class. There are moments like that that surpass the highest hopes and the boldest expectations.

Imagine middle school students who were fascinated with the primary campaigns of a presidential election year. Three very prominent Democrats—a governor, a senator, and a member of the House of Representatives—chose not to seek their party's nomination for president. The students create a fictional candidate named Governor Housesenate. The campaign theme song they wrote for this fictional candidate will be remembered decades later by the students and by their teacher. The teaching dream comes true and lives forever in cherished memories while being renewed today in classrooms where the good work that a teacher expected is surpassed by students who do great work, scholarly work, profound work, and work that means more to teachers than any formal award or career level ever could.

Creating a classroom trust level and the sense of mutual commitment of students and their teacher fosters the imagination, the creativity, the persistence, and the work ethic that makes the students part of the foundation that supports a teacher's dream. When a teacher and her students share the learning dream, they create a classroom reality together that leads to the dream.

18. The memories you did not realize would endure:

A student whom you taught years ago keeps in touch with you for decades. His career achievements make him a perfect guest speaker for your class. The classroom memories from when you taught him are vivid and are renewed when he speaks to your class. His superior presentation created new knowledge and new memories for everyone involved.

Another student whom you taught years ago has kept in touch. The letter from him was asking for prayerful support and financial support for a church mission trip he would take to Africa. It is an honor to support his journey. His letter strengthened precious memories of being his teacher. His mission trip created new memories as lives were touched in Africa.

A student whom you occasionally sent to the assistant principal's office sees you in a store years later. You both spoke precisely of the situation he had been involved in, the important lessons he had learned, and the proper discipline he was instilling in his sons now. His memories from years ago were becoming guidelines for his sons to know now and to apply throughout their lives.

The experiences cited above equal or exceed in quality and in meaning the lofty expectations of teachers who dream. It only takes a few parts of the teaching dream to come true occasionally for teachers to keep believing in and teaching toward the dream.

19. Exhaustion:

- "I never expected to be so tired after a day of teaching. I wonder if my teachers were this tired and I just never knew it."
- "There's something about being on your feet all day that exhausts your body. Then there's the emotional stress of dealing with groups of twenty-five or thirty students all day. By the end of school on Friday, I'm worn out every week."

- "I thought that, after a few years of teaching, I would get used to the physical demands. It never happened. I've taught for thirteen years and I think I'm pretty young, but my body is feeling older than my real age."
- "One other teacher who is never tired told me I work too hard. Well, I'm going to keep working the way I promised myself I would. If it means I get exhausted, well, I earned the exhaustion."

Take good care of heart, mind, body, and soul. Despite the claimed virtue of earned exhaustion, no person in any career does his or her best work when exhausted. Here is an example: rather than giving every one of your 140 high school students a long writing assignment due on the same day, stagger the long writing assignments across several due dates. You could also vary the length of assignments so some classes have longer writing tasks this week while other classes have academically valid, but shorter, writing tasks this week.

At certain times, take a walk, see a movie, visit a family friend who lives in a nursing home, take a nap, fix your favorite supper, call a friend, have a date with your spouse, play extra with your children, pray, read, and pursue your hobby; then get back to your very noble work.

20. Inspiration:

- "This is the best grade you have made on a test in our class. Great work. I'm proud of you."
- "You are welcome. It was a joy to be your teacher. It was an honor to write the letter of recommendation for you. Congratulations on the acceptances into great colleges and congratulations on your scholarships."
- "The questions you asked in our class were brilliant. You made all of us think, and that includes the teacher."
- "Thank you, thank you, thank you for nominating me for the Outstanding Teacher award. Your kind words in the nomination letter you wrote were very thoughtful and very inspiring."

The inspiring moments in a classroom include a brilliantly insightful answer from a student. Inspiring moments also include a student who struggled and struggled, yet finally, with encouragement from a teacher whose dream was implemented through persistence, masters the alphabet.

Inspirational moments bloom throughout the typical day in a school but are overlooked sometimes due to a preoccupation with the problems, the disappointments, the bureaucratic procedures, and the exhaustion. Notice the good. Celebrate the great. Absorb the energy of the inspirational moments that just might occur more often than is commonly realized.

21. *Isolation:*

In most cases, the teacher is the only adult in the classroom. A teacher's hours at school are spent with students by design. Most of the minutes a teacher spends with adults—other than in meetings or other scheduled events—must be arranged. Some teachers thrive on being independent educational entrepreneurs. Other teachers seem to prefer the company of adults than the classroom time with students. The reality of teaching time is that you, the one teacher in the classroom, do almost all of your work alone as far as other adults are concerned. If you prefer to work all day interacting with adults, teaching kindergarten through high school is not going to be your favorite place, and working in a school in any role as an educator will not be your favorite situation.

There are a few exceptions to the isolation of a teacher. A school administrator will visit your classroom two, three, four, or so times to formally observe you work. These two, three, four, or so limited observations are a significant portion of the information that leads to a conclusion about how well you are doing your work. First, do great work that always surpasses any and all parts of the observation data collection format and terminology. Second, keep the school administrators informed of your great work. Third, make copies of some of the work you or your students do in the 99 percent of the classroom time that you are not observed, and share that with the administrators.

The classroom where you are isolated from other adults is also the place where you can create the look, feel, and conditions. You are isolated from other adults, not from ideas, creativity, art, hope, wisdom, imagination, work, thinking, rules of proper conduct, rewards, celebrations, and much more. Design, arrange, organize, structure, and make your classroom into the dream classroom, and with your students the reality that is created can ascend toward the dream.

22. *What else?*

For readers who are preparing for a career in teaching, for readers who have accepted a teaching position and will begin their teaching career soon, and for people who are experienced with teaching, what other aspects of this work fit in the category—good or bad—of "teaching is not what you expect"? Please reflect on that topic; the space below can be used for your thoughts:

1.

2.

3.

4.

5.

6.

7.

8.

9.

10.

With a thorough analysis of the aspects of teaching that are not what is expected, we turn now to insights, certainties, truths, and teachers' wisdom of the ages.

Chapter Four

What Great Teachers Know About the Work of Great Teaching

During Paula Jordan's first year of teaching, she decided to quit teaching. Her hope was merely to survive one year and then to change careers so drastically that she would never see a classroom again.

Paula would apply to law school again. She kept asking herself, "What was I thinking? I was accepted to a great law school. That letter arrived during my senior year of college. I could be in law school right now instead of doing this teaching job. Why am I here instead of there? Why did I think I could do this job?"

There were reasons that had convinced Paula during her college years that she should become a teacher. She had worked for several summers at a girls' camp. She taught tennis at the camp, and she lived in a cabin with another counselor and fourteen middle school–age campers. Those were great summers. Paula's campers enjoyed camp, worked hard at their activities, and earned many honors. Several campers made amazing progress in tennis. The work at camp helped suggest for Paula that teaching could be perfect for her.

There were more reasons. During her teenage years, Paula did a lot of babysitting. There were three families in her neighborhood that relied on Paula to be a babysitter, to be almost a nanny, and as friendships grew over the years, to be a big sister to the children. Paula was comfortable with those roles, and she was very responsible with those obligations.

One of the families Paula babysat for included a mother who taught college classes in mathematics and a father who was a high school assistant principal. Everyone in that family told Paula that she would be a great teacher. College letters of recommendation from those two educators had helped Paula gain admission to her college and had helped her earn several scholarships.

Paula's grandmothers both had been teachers. When Paula was a child, she visited her grandparents often. Her grandfathers told her stories about World War II, and Paula was captivated. Her grandmothers would read books to Paula, and she was fascinated. Paula became an enthusiastic reader and thought how wonderful it would be to encourage students to read. The idea of becoming a teacher had a strong foundation by the time Paula began college and began selecting classes to take.

During high school, Paula was on the school's academic team, debate team, and tennis team. Her debating skills were superior. Her thinking ability and her communication ability in addition to the almost endless reading she did about how to excel in debating helped make her team the state champions in debate. So many people told her that she had the skills that lawyers must have. One of Paula's uncles is a lawyer, and he agreed she had all of the necessary skills for success as a lawyer.

Paula's mother and father own a computer store where computers are purchased, repaired, upgraded, and discussed. All possible technology gadgets are sold at the store. Paula has helped at the store for years. Her technology knowledge and skills are sophisticated. She has earned several technology certifications and could succeed in a career that applied those talents.

Still, with all of the experiences, opportunities, skills, and advice coming to Paula, there was something about teaching that most interested her and most inspired her. Paula had always liked school and had always done well in school. She had several outstanding teachers, and most of her other teachers were good. She could recall only one really bad teacher, and that person did not return to school after Christmas vacation due to, the official announcement diplomatically said, another career opportunity and some family matters. The truth was that the teacher just realized he was in the wrong job and nothing could change that fact. The next teacher was better, so everything seemed to work out for everyone.

"Should she pursue a career in teaching, law, or technology?" was the question that Paula thought about, got advice about, prayed about, thought about more, and then, at the end of her sophomore year of college, Paula made her decision. She would become a teacher; well, at least, she would design her college class schedules to earn certification as a teacher. She had been advised that it is much easier to gain that certification while she was in college than to do that after she graduated from college when the demands of life would become more complicated. She was told of alternative plans to teacher certification or of master's degrees that in one demanding calendar year resulted in teacher certification. Paula just thought it would be simpler to get this done while in college, and she really did expect to become a teacher.

In the spring semester of her senior year of college, Paula was ready to be a student teacher. In college, Paula had taken the classes she needed to become certified to teach any class about computers, math, and business. She had always taken an aggressive schedule of classes in each semester of college. If other people took four or five classes, Paula took five or six classes per semester. Her college years, she decided, were the one and only time she would have these opportunities. She was on the college debating club and played tennis in a league, but she was not on the college debate team or tennis team. She was a one-woman academic team who was earning a 3.8 grade-point average with two majors, computer science and math. She also was earning a minor in business. Plus she would be certified to teach computer, math, and business classes in middle school or high school.

Just to test the marketplace and possibly to have another option, Paula had applied to several law schools. On an especially difficult day of student teaching, Paula had a letter in her mailbox from a very respected law school. "Congratulations, Ms. Jordan. We are pleased to notify you of your acceptance into our law school." Paula almost called the law school immediately to accept the offer of admission, but she decided to wait a week.

During that week, she got some guidance from her college supervisor of student teaching and from the very experienced and accomplished high school math teacher she was working with. Paula was reassured as the next few days were better than the one especially difficult day, but she wondered if her perception of teaching was too idealistic. Lawyers probably have very difficult days, too, she thought, and she found herself increasingly leaning toward teaching.

In April of her senior year of college, as student teaching was concluding, the math teacher Paula was working with announced her retirement after thirty years of teaching. Paula was encouraged to apply for this math teaching job. She did apply, and she was selected for the job on May 3, one week before her graduation from college and four days before the law school deadline for acceptance of the admission offer. There was more thinking to do.

As Paula listened to advice from her family, her professors, teachers at the high school where she was a student teacher, friends, and career counselors, she realized how fortunate she was to have the job offer and the law school opportunity. Both possibilities seemed to be very good. Which one was better for Paula Jordan?

There was no dramatic moment when a clear sign of what to do appeared. There was no flip of a coin with "heads, I teach; tails, I go to law school." There was no dream of a classroom or of a courtroom that Paula awakened from with complete certainty knowing what to do.

What convinced Paula to accept the teaching job was that, at age twenty-two, she had been preparing for this throughout half of her life. When she was eleven years old, she taught games to children in the neighborhood, and when she was thirteen years old, she began babysitting for some of those children. She had many good experiences working at the camp with middle school students. Student teaching has its difficult days but had improved a lot in the final weeks as Paula made the necessary adjustments to do what worked with her students instead of doing what sounded good on a teaching methodology paper she wrote during her junior year of college. Paula had been on a path toward teaching for eleven years. It was time to see where that path would lead her as she went into a high school math teaching job.

It was awful. It was not merely difficult, challenging, frustrating, tiring, or bad. It was awful. Paula's three classes of geometry had thirty-one or thirty-two students each. Her two classes of Algebra I had twenty-nine or thirty students each. One hundred and fifty-three students turning in math homework two or three times each week meant 306 or 459 homework papers to grade weekly. Tests would be additional grading. The classes she worked with as a student teacher had twenty-three to twenty-five students. What explained the higher numbers? Paula was told that the school was encouraging more students to take geometry. She also found out that many ninth-grade students had failed Algebra I last year, so the numbers in those classes were up as students took Algebra I again.

The years of babysitting or of working at the camp had not provided Paula with the skills needed to teach math to so many students who were two or three years below grade and who struggle with basic arithmetic. Paula was also not trained in dealing with so many students who were addicted to their cell phones, which they were determined to find ways to use during class, to homework not getting turned in, to cheating and copying on tests, to intentional and repeated tardiness to class, to vulgar language in class, and to severe selfishness by students who refused to learn and whose disruptions limited what the eager-to-learn students could accomplish.

Paula did everything she knew to do. She wrote discipline referrals. She rewarded students who did behave and who did turn in work. She spoke with parents and guardians. She got advice from the school administrators and school counselors. She asked other teachers for ideas. She called her college professors. She talked with the math teacher whose retirement had created this job opening, and she asked some students for their ideas.

Nothing worked as well as Paula hoped. Babysitting had been so enjoyable. The camp counselor experiences were wonderful. Student teaching had gone from difficult to productive as Paula made the necessary changes. Nothing was working now. Paula decided that, to establish control over the class, she would have to use more and more worksheets of math problems, which students were to do silently at their desk. She also called the office whenever a student caused a disruption until, after nine students were removed from her classes in one week, the other students would now walk in, sit down, complete the worksheet, remain quiet, and leave when the bell rang. This was awful. This was not teaching. Paula wondered what first-year law school students were doing.

During Christmas vacation, Paula's high school's basketball teams were involved in tournaments. The girls' team was hosting an eight-team tournament. The boy's team was in an adjacent county participating in an eight-team tournament. Paula went to all of the games in both tournaments that her school's teams played. Why go to those games? It was the only action Paula had not taken. Maybe students would appreciate her interest in the school's basketball teams and start cooperating with her. Maybe she could find something in basketball that could apply to math class. She knew the students talked about sports a lot, so maybe some way could be found to connect sports and math. Paula's boyfriend, Thomas Marion, went to the games with her, so it would be a good way for them to be together and get away from Paula's routine of always doing schoolwork and her boyfriend's routine of always doing schoolwork as he was completing his MBA this year. When the school year ended, he would start working for a large regional bank's headquarters in the same city where he and Paula had gone to college, where he was in graduate school, and where she was teaching.

The basketball games were enjoyable and exciting. The girls' team won their championship game by two points as one of Paula's students hit two free throws with one second left on the clock. The boys lost their championship game by six points.

Paula saw many students at the games. Almost all of her students whom she saw spoke politely to her. They seemed to be very appreciative that a teacher would come to the games. Everyone was impressed that Paula was there with Thomas. It reminded Paula that students sometimes think that teachers live at school and have no life, friends, or family anywhere else.

Paula wondered why the students who cause so many problems in her classroom were friendly to her at the basketball games. She noticed that students who rarely if ever pay attention in class were paying complete attention to every moment of each basketball game. She was especially interested that two of her students who were very lazy in math class and barely made passing grades were working relentlessly on the basketball court.

Thomas and Paula discussed the basketball games, the students, and the math classes. Thomas thought that the difference was the students could actually experience basketball, so it was real to them. Math seemed like something that adults thought was important, so the students gave it less attention.

Paula questioned Thomas, "But don't they see the math in basketball? The score is numbers, the statistics about the game; that's all math."

Thomas had an idea. "Maybe you just solved your problem, Paula. Use basketball statistics to teach math. Why did the girls' team win? Was it their free throw percentage, their three-point shot percentage, the number of turnovers they caused, or some other statistic? What did the boys do better in the games they won versus the game they lost? Show your students how math explains basketball. Use sports situations to teach the geometry and the algebra."

"But, Thomas, not all of the students like sports. Maybe I can make a variety of math stuff: math for athletes; math for musicians; math for people who like movies, television, or video games; math for students who like cars; and money math. It's worth a try. Nothing else has worked. Thanks for the suggestion."

"You are welcome, Paula. It's straight from my MBA classes. The most successful businesses listen to customers. At these basketball games, you learned a lot about your students by listening to them and watching them."

On the first school day in January after Christmas vacation, Paula distributed a sports statistics analysis set of facts, calculations, equations, formulas, and problems. As the students realized this was not just one more typical worksheet, some of them got curious. As the students realized that all of the statistics came from their school's recent basketball games, they became interested. As they saw a newspaper sports story with names of their friends who were on the teams and with statistics about the games, the classroom started to feel just a little bit like the camp where Paula had such good experiences as a counselor.

The task was to analyze the statistics and determine which factor led to basketball victories. In the games the boys won, their field goal shooting percentage was 48 percent or better. In the game they lost, their field goal shooting percentage was 37 percent. In the games they won, they committed, on the average, fewer fouls than in the game they lost.

For the girls, in each of their tournament wins, they clearly out-rebounded the other teams, and they scored more points from free throws than the other teams. One girl in Ms. Jordan's second-period class who is on the basketball team asked if she could go tell her coach right now about these statistics. Ms. Jordan was concerned about interrupting that teacher's class, but she wanted to keep the student's excitement building.

"While everyone finishes the last few problems, come over to my computer, Tasha. You and I can send your coach an e-mail so we don't interrupt her class. Then you can tell her more later." That worked well, and the student came to class the next day with a story about how the team discussed the statistics at practice and she led the discussion.

Paula had to smile as she thought, "Nothing like this is going on in any first-year law school class today." Paula would have been a conscientious and successful law school student. She could have been a superior lawyer. During the first semester of her first year of teaching, Paula had taken the law school admissions test, and her score was better than when she took that test as a college senior. She had applied to law school again during those darkest days of that awful first semester.

The second semester had a few dark days. There are just some days, Paula concluded, when a teacher does everything possible and a student insists on being disruptive, defiant, disorderly, or vulgar. Paula had decided to quit blaming herself when a student intentionally disobeyed. One assistant principal told her,

> It's like the police. Do they blame themselves when somebody commits a crime? No, the police do all they can to maintain safety, but some people commit crimes anyway. You are doing everything a person can do for these students. Most of them are cooperating with you now. Keep working with all of them, but for a high school student who has been in school already for ten years or so to cause problems, that student is causing trouble on purpose. They know the rules just like criminals know the law, but some people try to see what they can get away with.

Paula was admitted to law school for the second time. She felt awkward saying no, because she knew how many people get rejected by law school. In saying no to the law school for a second time, she was saying yes for a second time to teaching. She was beginning to think that this was a permanent yes to teaching.

As Paula completed her first year of teaching and signed a contract to return for a second year, she was thankful for all she had learned and that the second semester had been so much better than the first semester. Her teaching schedule for the second year was two classes of geometry, two classes of Algebra I, and one new class that she had created. The new class was a semester of sports statistics followed by a semester of money math. Paula had become convinced that the place to begin with students who do poorly in math is with the math they already care about, use daily, and understand. Sports statistics and money math would include all math curriculum standards for ninth-grade math, including algebra. These classes were among the many reasons that Paula would return for a second year.

Paula had decided that the students needed her, that the school needed her, and that teaching needed her. Paula had decided with equal conviction that she needed teaching, she needed to work in a school, and that she needed to work with students. She could see herself doing this work for many years, many challenging and fascinating years.

Paula Marion was completing her tenth year of teaching. Thomas Marion and Paula Jordan were married in the summer following her second year of teaching and his first year of working in the bank office. After ten years of teaching and eight years of marriage, Paula was content. She and Thomas had a six-year-old son, Robert, and a four-year-old daughter, Julie.

Thomas was now a vice president of the bank. Paula had earned two graduate school degrees that expanded her credentials to include certification

as a school counselor, certification as a school principal or assistant principal, and certification as a school curriculum supervisor. Her graduate school
work also included many classes about very complex and advanced mathematics. She also took a class in the business of sports marketing that gave her
many practical math ideas to use with her students. For now, Paula intended
to continue teaching, but when her children were a few years older, she
planned to seriously consider becoming a school counselor or an assistant
principal.

Paula's eleventh year of teaching began well, in part because her reputation with students was clearly established. Students said of Mrs. Marion,

- "She'll do anything for you."
- "She's great. She means business, but she's cool."
- "The best teacher and she's the toughest teacher."
- "It's a neat class, but do the work. She'll never let you just get by."

Paula's teaching schedule for her eleventh year included the improved version of sports statistics plus money math. This yearlong class for ninth graders or tenth graders was called Real Math Now. The class incorporates all
aspects of Algebra I, some introduction concepts of geometry, and mastery of
basic arithmetic. There is no textbook for the class. Paula created the materials that will be used. She will create new materials throughout the year as
teaching opportunities arise from economic data, sports statistics, questions
from students about taxes or other money matters, and situations at school
such as budget of the school or the cost of the prom.

The eleventh year of teaching would include Paula's first opportunity to
teach a dual-credit class. High school seniors would take this advanced math
class to earn a high school credit and to earn three hours of college credit.
This would be Paula Marion's first class each day, and twice weekly the class
began thirty minutes before the high school instructional days. This extra
time was required for all students in the dual-credit class to provide the
necessary time to learn math at the college level.

During the summer after her eleventh year of teaching, Paula was asked
to speak at a state conference of math teachers. The conference planners had
heard of Paula's Real Math Now class and had decided that all math teachers
at the conference could benefit from knowing about this class. The text of
Paula's presentation at the math conference follows along with the question-
and-answer comments that involved Mrs. Marion and other math teachers.

MAKING MATH REAL NOW

Thank you for the invitation to participate as a speaker at our state's annual conference of math teachers. It is much to the credit of our math teacher association that these conferences emphasize the very practical approach of teachers sharing good ideas with each other and teachers listening to each other to find answers to questions of mutual concern.

I recently completed my eleventh year of teaching at Summit High School in Adamson County. I'll be honest, years ago during my first semester of teaching, I was almost at the point of leaving this profession forever. Now, it looks as though I will remain in this profession forever.

What changed? It became obvious to me that many students think that they hate math, yet many of those same students do not realize how much they also need math, use math, and sometimes like math. That sounds contradictory, but here is an example: word problems. How many students hate word problems? If you think that most students hate word problems, raise your hands, please. Amazing. Notice that some of you raised both hands, and a few of you stood up for emphasis. You are right. Most students hate word problems, especially the dreaded two trains left the station problem.

All of us know that many essential thinking skills are activated by solving word problems, so student hatred of word problems cannot be a reason for math teachers to give up on word problems. Many students love sports. Could love of sports be a way to reduce hatred of word problems? My experience with the Real Math Now class I teach says that the answer is yes.

Imagine this conversation between three high school students. I have recruited two colleagues from my school to help me present this teenage conversation. Please imagine that the three of us are high school students, and listen closely as we discuss some very important sports topics.

Hannah: It's the district tournament. Don't you realize what that means? We have to win our district to get to the regional tournament. Then we have to win the region to get to the state. We've been working on this since we were in the ninth grade. It's our senior year. It's our last chance.

Levi: I know. The soccer tournaments begin next week. The plan was always for the girls' team and the boys' team to get to the state tournament our senior year. I was stupid to let my grades drop and stuff. I have two days to get those Fs up to Cs or I'm not eligible.

Steven: What have you been doing? Since when did Levi the brain ever make an F in anything? Did you try to make Fs?

Hannah: No, he did not try, well, not really. He has that part-time job at the grocery store. He has that high-maintenance, full-time girlfriend. He plays soccer, well up until today. So, Levi just quit studying. I've seen you in physics class. You sleep or do nothing.

Levi: It's not that bad. I just have to get the physics grade up and my English grade up. Nothing to it. It's just tests to make up and other stuff to do.

Steven: Have you finished the math for tomorrow? Didn't you sign up for the math of soccer project? Have you analyzed all of these soccer statistics?

Levi: Oh, well, I mean . . .

Hannah: You haven't done anything have you? It's soccer statistics. You've played soccer forever. Can't you keep up with a math project that is about soccer? I did my project on the math of paying for college. It is so expensive. I'm applying for every scholarship that exists. I never knew college costs so much. Books are like one thousand dollars per year. Just for some dumb books.

Steven: Books that cost that much aren't dumb, just expensive. I did my project on the math of part-time jobs. I found out that I can make more money fixing computers, cutting grass, shoveling snow, and babysitting than I can at the grocery store. People ask me for computer help all the time. My neighbors need yard work done. Yard work is so easy. It takes an hour or so, and I get thirty dollars to cut a yard. Babysitting is easy money. We play games, we do computer stuff, we do our homework, and I feed the children I babysit if they need it. Ten dollars an hour and the families give big tips.

Hannah: Levi, don't just stand here in the hall. You've got time before first-period class, so go get caught up in your classes. Oh, no, here comes your girlfriend. You'll never get that physics done. Can you ever say no to her?

Steven: There they go. The answer must be no. He never says no to her. He should go do physics. Doesn't she understand that? Wait. Why are they coming back here?

Levi: Hey, we're going to the library. I'm going to get that physics done. Elizabeth said I had to do the work right now. Some guys on the soccer team asked her to be sure I get my grades up. See you.

Hannah: Can you believe that? Maybe I was wrong about her. If Elizabeth gets Levi to get those grades to C or better, she's all right.

Steven: Speaking of grades, what did you find out about grades and college? You know, do they really look at your grades?

Hannah: Mostly I looked at the costs of college. It is bad and gets worse each year. I did see some stuff about the tests you have to take and why a 3.0 B average is important, but an A average is a lot better. I did read that colleges expect us to take tough classes our senior year in high school and make good grades. I changed my schedule for the second semester to get out of that easy class I have and to quit being an office aide. I signed up for an advanced U.S. history class that is just about the twentieth century. And I signed up for a one-semester Shakespeare class. The teacher promised me that I would think Shakespeare was writing plays today the way we would study it.

Steven: Maybe. Does the teacher think Levi and Elizabeth are the modern Romeo and Juliet?

Hannah: I don't know about that, but maybe modern things like how dating has now changed from a long time ago are parts of the class. Hey, I need to get to class. See you at lunch.

Steven: Yeah. See ya. Should I quote Shakespeare to impress you?

Hannah: If you get Levi to improve his grades that will impress me more.

Many thanks to my math teaching colleagues Samuel Edom and John Bethesda for helping me present that skit by playing the roles of Levi and Steven. Thanks, also, to Rachael Davidson, the president of our math teachers association, for playing the part of Elizabeth. Now, let's think of what we know about the three students whose conversation we heard. What do we know about Hannah, Levi, and Steven? Also, what do we know about Elizabeth. Please, just walk up to a microphone in either aisle, and tell us your thoughts.

Speaker 1: We know that Levi is going to work hard enough to get to play soccer.

Speaker 2: We know that students like to talk to each other.

Speaker 3: We know that, using math, Hannah now knows how expensive college will be. That assignment really got her attention. She learned more than she expected to.

Speaker 4: Steven's math project showed him the best ways to make money.

Speaker 5: We know that Hannah was willing to take harder classes when she found out on her own that it mattered to colleges if she took hard classes her senior year. She had probably been told that by her parents or her school counselor, but she took it serious when she found out on her own.

Speaker 6: We know that Hannah was way too quick to judge Elizabeth.

Speaker 7: We learned that students can have a lot on their minds.

Thanks for those comments. I would combine all of your thoughts into this statement: students are real people living real lives right now. Because soccer matters right now, doing the physics and English work had to matter to Levi right now.

I would suggest to you that the timed-release approach to education is not convincing and is not inspiring. We tell elementary school students to work hard so they will be well prepared for middle school. We tell middle school students to work hard so they will be ready for high school. What do we tell high school students? We tell them to work hard and learn a lot so they will be ready for college. To students who keep hearing those statements they must wonder why can't what we do in school matter to my life right now.

The answer in the Real Math Now classroom is that what we do in school today can and does matter to your life right now. Every student I have taught has had some wholesome interest that could connect with math. Sports, part-time job, money, cars, career plans, singing, theater, coin collecting, travel, video games, computers, food, and so much more. Math and math skill development connect with all of those good interests. So, I get to know enough about my students to see what they bring to the classroom that we can connect math to. It works, largely, I think, because students—remember, they are real people living real lives right now—can see the use of Real Math Now right now in their lives today.

My students work many math problems, do homework, complete problems on the board in class, take quizzes, and take tests. Real Math Now is real work and lots of it. I do not hear complaints about the workload because the work matters to students right now.

Last year, I talked to some of my students who played football. One of my classes happened to have a lot of football players in it. My question was why they endure getting blocked, getting tackled, getting worn out, running drills, and feeling the aches and pains? They said those things did not hurt as much as winning football games felt good. For them, football matters right now. Football to them is real and it is real now.

It has been my experience that, when math becomes real now, the students make a commitment to doing the math work now. Real Math Now matters and gets results in ways that "two trains left the station" math can never reach. Now, we have time for a few questions, so feel free to come to a microphone and ask.

Speaker 1: What do you do to convince people that Real Math Now class includes all of the required curriculum and math skills for the grade level?

Paula: That is so important. Some people might think that Real Math is just fun and games designed to play with math. In my classroom, all of the math curriculum content and standards are posted for each high school grade level. Each student has a copy of the curriculum content and standards. All students have to document their successful completion of three Real Math activities that confirm mastery of each part of the curriculum. Then, there are tests that students are given to confirm again that they are mastering the standards. I create the tests. I grade the tests. I know, day to day, with the activities and interactions in class, with the student-compiled evidence of mastery, and with the tests, where each student stands in terms of each part of the math curriculum.

Speaker 2: How much time does it take to create your Real Math Now activities? If each student is interested in something different, that would be a lot of material for you to create.

Paula: To be honest, it does take a lot of time. The good news is that it gets results. The time is efficient. If you distribute worksheet after worksheet of "two trains left the station" type of problems, you do not get the same results my students and I get with Real Math. Sometimes, the students design the materials. I could give them the advertising inserts from the Sunday newspaper detailing sales at several grocery stores or computer stores. They have to create math problems that practice, demonstrate, or apply certain skills. I would rather invest time in making or designing materials that get results than copying worksheets that do not get results.

Speaker 3: What do school administrators think of your methods?

Paula: They see many ninth graders passing math class, maybe making A or B grades in math class, and very rarely but sometimes, a few students getting in trouble in math class, so, overall, they are pleased. My overall methods were presented to and approved by our school's curriculum committee many years ago. It is important to follow procedures like that. I invite the school administrators to visit my classes; I send them copies of the math work we are doing. They know the math is not just real to the students; it is real math content, skills, and curriculum.

I want to thank everyone for your wonderful attention during this presentation. Thank you for your questions. You have been given a handout with some samples of activities that my students have done in recent years. Those handouts include my e-mail and my Web page on our schools' website. Please keep in touch with me so we can trade ideas. One of the best resources in our profession is each other, so let's work together in person when possible, electronically when necessary. Now, go make math more real than ever for your students.

The years were good to Thomas Marion and Paula Marion. They had much to be thankful for. Thomas reached his career goal of bank president. Paula also reached a career goal of being a school counselor at Summit High School. As she completed her twenty-third year at Summit, an assistant principal position became open when a colleague of Paula's retired. Paula applied for and was selected for that school administrator position. Paula and Thomas were the proud parents of their nineteen-year-old son, Robert, who had just completed his first year of college, and their seventeen-year-old daughter, Julie, who had completed her junior year of high school and could not wait to be a high school senior.

Just before the start of her first year as an assistant principal, Paula met with her principal, Brian Alexander, to seek his advice. She was ready to do the job, and she shared Julie's "cannot wait for school to start" attitude. Her question was about how to most effectively work with teachers. Brian had sound advice to offer.

That is important, very important. You work in the same school building as teachers, but your assistant principal's job is completely different from a teacher's job. You saw some differences between teaching and being a school counselor, but the work you did with students as their counselor did have some teaching elements to it. You will notice in your assistant principal work that there are fewer and fewer similarities in your new job description and in a teacher's job description.

Still, you can use a lot of your teacher insights and instincts. Some of your time each day needs to be spent in classrooms. Do as much of that as possible. The tasks you must do in your new job sometimes cannot wait or seem to pile up—discipline incidents, parents and guardians who have to meet with you and who just show up, mechanical problems in the building, bus loading and unloading supervision, cafeteria supervision, hallway supervision, and paperwork. Make time to get into classrooms so you see what teachers and students are doing. The heart of a school is not here in the office. The heart of a school is in the classrooms.

You asked about how to work with teachers. I would suggest that it could work well if you apply your Real Math Now ideas. For example, when you officially observe a teacher for purposes of the school district's annual, formal evaluation, emphasize the full range of the teacher's work, not just the few hours you spend observing several classes taught by that teacher. Teachers will tell you that the evaluation system is not a real measure of all they do. How can we see all they do if we only visit their classroom three times in a year and use those three observations as the basis of our evaluation?

Beware of those mini-observations, though. A few years ago, you may recall, our school district had that system of four-minute walk-through observations. Teachers hated those. A principal or assistant principal would come to a class, observe for a few minutes, fill out a short checklist form, and put a copy of the form in the teacher's mailbox. That was 100 percent bureaucratic. It was so superficial. You can and should thoroughly visit classrooms often.

If you are observing a teacher officially this year, meet with the teacher in August or September. Let them know you will visit often for fifteen, twenty, or thirty minutes. Let them know you will visit at least three times to observe an entire class. Ask the teacher to send you a copy of tests her students take, materials they are given to read, and anything else she wants you to know about during the year. Make the observation and evaluation process thorough, human, and, to use one of your favorite words, real. This way observation is not some bureaucratic agony we impose on teachers. This way it becomes the type of partnership you always developed with your students.

Do keep in mind that adults are different from students. We are dealing with a job, a career, a life's work, when we interact with teachers. Still, how we interact with teachers makes a big difference in what administrators can accomplish with teachers. Does all of that make sense?

Paula paused before answering. She was thinking about the past twenty-three years of teaching and of school counselor work. "Oh, yes, it makes sense. I was just realizing that few things matter more in this profession, whatever the exact job may be, than how we treat each other. Maybe education gets too political and complicated and bureaucratic. It's mostly about people and being, oh, being real with them. Thanks for your good advice."

In November of the school year, Paula was increasingly confident she was mastering the duties of being an assistant principal. She kept up with the daily tasks that were predictable in general but not in specifics. Some students were sent to the office each day for misbehaviors. A few of those students were in trouble once or twice a week. Others were in trouble once or twice and never again.

Paula spent time each day in classrooms. There were eighteen teachers whom she would officially evaluate this year. She made sure to visit each of those eighteen classrooms twice per week. As she monitored hallways before school or at class change times, she talked with teachers, staff members, and students, always making an extra effort to see any of the eighteen teachers she would formally observe and evaluate. She was determined to have a complete awareness of the work that each of those eighteen teachers did in their classroom.

In February, Paula had completed the three official classroom observations with those eighteen teachers. She had invested much time with these teachers, observing three classes from start to finish, but also including many other discussions, short but meaningful visits, and reading materials teachers gave her about the work being done in their classrooms. It was now time to have a comprehensive meeting to review the overall observation process with each teacher individually.

Paula met with Emmanuel Bristol, a physics and chemistry teacher, during Mr. Bristol's planning period. The discussion emphasized the depth of knowledge that Mr. Bristol established as the standard in his classroom. Mr. Bristol took science very seriously. He had turned down some lucrative science research job offers when he had accepted the teaching job at Summit High School three years ago. Mr. Bristol was known as a conscientious, caring, no-nonsense teacher.

Paula was surprised when she had completed presenting to Mr. Bristol a very favorable evaluation and she heard an unexpected comment. Mr. Bristol and Mrs. Marion had spent time during the year discussing how well his students were doing and how productive his classes were. The discussion, so far, this morning had continued that very favorable tone. Mrs. Marion stated that she could confidently give Mr. Bristol the highest evaluation, which was termed "superior." Emmanuel expressed his appreciation for Paula's confidence in his work, but then he said the unexpected: "It might be time for me to change jobs. Actually, it is time for me to change jobs, I think. These three years of high school teaching have been good, but it's harder and harder to see myself doing this for the next twenty-five or thirty years."

Paula's thoughts raced back to the first semester of her first year of teaching. That had been awful. Mr. Bristol's classes at this school had been good for his three years as far as Paula knew. He had every reason to be proud of his work as a teacher. His students learned and behaved well. There had been no indications of job dissatisfaction by Mr. Bristol.

Paula replied, "I'm sorry to hear that. I hope we can work together to correct whatever is wrong. You are a good teacher, a superior teacher. Your students learn a lot of science. I've seen that happen day after day. What could be done here at school to change whatever is not working for you?"

Mr. Bristol was honest. "Nothing. I do teach well. My students do learn. I put in a lot of extra time and effort because I expect that of myself. I make thirty-eight thousand dollars per year. Three years ago, I turned down jobs that paid twice that much. The highest pay level for a teacher in our school district is sixty-three thousand dollars, and that is for someone with twenty-nine years of experience and a doctorate degree. I have a job offer right now that would pay me more than the highest teacher pay in our district. I am married. We have a child on the way. The financial responsibilities I have toward my family are growing. I cannot fulfill those responsibilities the way I think I should with a teacher's salary."

Paula offered some ideas. "There are additional duties that pay. You could coach a sport. You could sponsor a club. You could teach summer school."

"Paula, doing all of that means forty-four thousand dollars instead of thirty-eight thousand dollars. My wife dreams of being a stay-at-home mother. I can make that happen for her. The company that has offered me a laboratory research job can pay me more, give me benefits that no school can give, offer me stock in the company, pay an annual bonus, help fund my retirement savings plan, and help fund a college savings plan. I'm twenty-five years old. I'm young enough to make a career change and have several decades to advance. This company will not keep me in the same job for thirty years. I will get promoted. I will advance and someday be an officer in the company with a superior reputation in the scientific community. The company will pay for me to go to graduate school and will fit my work schedule around my graduate school schedule because they do so much with the university. I have to do this. I'll miss the school and the students, but this is right for my family."

Paula had not planned for their meeting to include this discussion. "Mr. Bristol, you are a superior teacher. If you stay in teaching, you'll just keep getting better and better. I understand everything you said, and I respect your commitment to your family. Obviously, you have given this much thought. Be sure to talk with Mr. Alexander."

"I have. We spoke before school this morning. I knew that we would meet today, so I wanted to inform the principal first and then you."

There was nothing else to say. Mr. Bristol and Mrs. Marion smiled, shook hands, signed the evaluation forms, and concluded their meeting.

The career reality, the financial reality, the job marketplace reality, and the classroom reality all intersected in Mr. Bristol's decision. By all accounts, Emmanuel Bristol is a great teacher. He knows science. He knows how to teach science to high school students. He knows how to manage his classroom, actually his laboratory. He had enough of a dream to teach that he turned down scientific research jobs three years ago so he could be a teacher.

During those three years, life has changed for Mr. Bristol. Marriage and a child to be born in a few months are different dreams with their unique realities. Mr. Bristol can change jobs, double his pay, and provide for his family according to their dream.

Paula thought of what life would have been like if she had practiced law for the past twenty years. She knew that she would have a been a very good lawyer but that something would have been missing. What she sought from her career could be found only in a school. Once that first semester many years ago had been survived, learned from, and changed, Paula knew that she belonged in schoolwork. For all the difficulties within every school, there were daily opportunities for amazing results. Classroom results meant more to Paula than courtroom results.

Lawyers should be lawyers; teachers should be teachers. In a perfect world, Mr. Bristol could keep being a great teacher and could care for his family as he intended to. Paula knew that schools are not perfect and that schools do not function in a perfect world. Still, it really bothered her that students for the next thirty years would not be taught by Emmanuel Bristol. There had to be a better way.

It took a lot of work, but Paula made phone call after phone call. She was given ample support by her principal and by officials in her school district. The idea was an educational triangle combining the school district, the university, and local companies. Paula invited people from those three groups to meet and explore ways that very talented teachers could work with university professors on joint venture projects that the university and companies had established already or could establish. Paula envisioned paid summer work opportunities for teachers who, during six summer weeks, would work with university professors and corporate partners. It could be scientific research. It could be mathematical analysis of business data. It could be world language instruction for corporate employers or other international endeavors supported with cultural and language knowledge.

The interest level was high. The university knew the value of working with high school teachers whose students could then learn from their teachers more about the opportunities at the university in their hometown. The local companies were eager to support education, and they could see the benefits of paying for six weeks of work for one or more teachers as a way to advance corporate projects that needed concentrated effort rather than continuous effort. This could help some of the companies manage their seasonal human resources needs while also giving attention to creative long-term, business-building projects that had much merit but did not always get done in the urgent pace of dealing with the daily emergencies in a corporation.

It might take a year or more of planning, but Paula was determined to get the educational triangle started. That program could help schools keep some great teachers who seek higher pay, who seek additional learning experiences for themselves, who have an interest in workplaces other than schools yet who would like to continue teaching, and who are eager to work in June and July. The program also had benefits for students, for the university, and for local companies.

Although she was now an assistant principal, Paula intended to do her current job with the same creativity, persistence, heart, and soul that had made her a great teacher. Part of what great teachers know about the work of great teaching is that what made them a great teacher can be applied throughout a school and throughout a school district to help create great schools and great school districts.

Paula was still disappointed that students would not be taught by Mr. Bristol, but she hoped that some teachers who participated in the educational triangle program could work with Mr. Bristol as he advanced his career with a local company. Paula had made sure that Mr. Bristol's company was a participant in the educational triangle board of directors.

The disappointing reality of Mr. Bristol having to leave teaching had given Mrs. Marion the reasons she needed to begin a new dream, the educational triangle. Great teachers believe that to every challenging reality in education there can be an equal and opposite dream.

Paula Marion, assistant principal, had spent more time during August through February observing for five full class periods and for shorter visits two or three times weekly in Katy Vermont's classroom. Paula had completed all of the postobservation conferences with seventeen of the eighteen teachers she was evaluating this year. Paula was encouraged that, of those seventeen, all but one could be evaluated as good or superior. Paula expected all of those seventeen teachers to return to Summit High School except for Mr. Bristol. Then there was Katy Vermont.

Katy was an amazingly talented person. Her hobbies included white-water rafting, snow skiing, mountain climbing, triathlons, and gardening. She was certified to teach middle school and high school art classes in addition to middle school and high school English classes. Her love for art and her love for literature convinced her to double major in those subjects during college while also getting certified to teach both of those areas. Katy completed all of that college work in three and a half years, while keeping two part-time jobs and staying healthy enough to run in two marathons per year during college. Katy is an amazing person.

Katy has been teaching for thirteen years. She began with middle school art and taught that for seven years. Then she decided a change would be beneficial so she has taught high school English for six years. When visiting Katy's classroom for a full class period or for a shorter time, Paula always saw a perfectly designed room. Katy's art talent meant that the classroom walls were covered with her original works of art, many of which related to scenes in the works of literature her students read.

There were days when Katy's teaching was outstanding. Then there were days when the teaching was ordinary. Never was there a time when the teaching was unprofessional or unacceptable, but Paula wondered why a person of Katy's ability, energy, creativity, and skill would ever settle for ordinary or average. After some pleasant conversation about classroom art, Paula began the conference with Katy with a neutral question: "Katy, how is this year going for you?"

Katy paused. Katy's pause lingered. Paula almost repeated her question but Katy shook her head to communicate that asking the question once was ample. "It's okay. It's just okay. And I really hate okay. I did not enter this profession thirteen years ago to be an okay teacher or an average teacher. I intended to be great, and I have been great. I still am great sometimes, but more often I am just okay in the classroom. I hope you have some good ideas for me.

"I know that I comply with everything on the evaluation form. I do what is required at the very least. My work is never below the okay or satisfactory level according to every evaluation I have had, but I'm not satisfied with being a satisfactory teacher. I hated those old report cards in elementary school that said I was satisfactory in handwriting or spelling or anything. Satisfactory just blends in. I want to stand out, not blend in. What do you think, Mrs. Marion?"

Paula had prepared some conclusions to share with Katy, so she went through all of those. "Your classroom looks magnificent. The art creates an intellectual atmosphere. Your lessons are organized well with clear objectives that you state and that you write on the board. You use a variety of teaching activities, and the students seemed to be aware of what you required."

"Excuse me, Mrs. Marion. I know all of that. What I don't know is how to be a great teacher every day like I used to be."

Paula asked, "What do you think changed? On the days when you are not doing the great teaching you expect of yourself, what is different?"

Katy had thought about this enough to have an exact answer. "That's easy. Teaching now is just not like it was ten years ago or thirteen years ago when I started. The high school seniors I have now were five years old when I started teaching. What kind of education did they get or not get that brought them to my classes so unprepared to work, to really work with a serious eagerness to learn? Most of them seem so distracted, so apathetic. Their part-time job, their computer games, their cell phones, their romances, and their sports get most of their effort. Then I get complaints from their parents about why I let their son or daughter fail or barely pass. I do all I know to do. I call parents. I mail updated grade reports to them. I e-mail them. Teaching is just not what it used to be.

"And something else. Schools cannot solve every problem that children and teenagers have. There just is not an education solution to every problem that young people face. From fighting obesity to stopping Internet bullying, and from preparing all students for college—even the students who will fail high school class after class—to doing social work for students, teachers and schools are asked, no told, to deal with every need that every student has. It makes no sense to ask educators to be social workers, psychologists, physi-cians, and pharmacists—can you believe how many students take medica-tions at school—well, it's too much. It's just way too much. It means being an ordinary teacher because I'm forced to do so much nonteaching work."

"Katy, not all of the days this year have been ordinary. I've been in your classes enough to see good work or even great work. What is being done on those days to get better results?" Paula was hoping that some Socratic ques-tioning would enable Katy to discover the reality within her classroom for herself. The process required only a few questions.

"I have thought about that enough to figure it out. The best days are when we do something with art, music, or food. Art could be anything from a short children's cartoon we watch to the most sophisticated book cover design that the students create to go with a story they wrote. Music, which I tell them is audio art, is used in class to see the impact of notes plus lyrics versus just lyrics. And with food, it's not eating stuff in class; it's some creative writing such as 'create the conversation between a chocolate chip cookie and choco-late ice cream as they debate which of them is a better version of chocolate.'

"On the other days, we do the routine stuff, which the state and the school district and the school curriculum committee tell us we have to do—vocabu-lary, sentence structure, types of writing, more vocabulary, grammar rules and uses, and other requirements. When we have to just wade through, it makes all of us ordinary."

Paula knew the answer. "Katy, you already answered your own question. Think again about the great days and the ordinary days. What is different?"

"Well, on the great days, we have art, music, or food. On the ordinary days, we do the ordinary work that is required."

"Right, Katy. Think about that. Not just what you are doing on the differ-ent days but how you are doing it. How much art or music or food do you use when you and your students are doing the required work?"

Katy was getting hopeful. "Well, I always follow the curriculum. We complete everything that is required. It's those paint-by-numbers mandates we get more of each year. The set of twenty vocabulary lists we are given that students have to master. We get three lesson plans to use, and they are always dull."

One more question might be enough. Paula asked, "About those lesson plans. What can you or any teacher ask for?"

Silence followed by a smile followed by the answer. "Well, you are right, Mrs. Marion. I can ask for an exemption. I can create alternative lessons, and the curriculum committee might approve them. Why didn't I think of that? I probably know why. I just got really resentful of the bureaucrats in some office sending us all of these mandates and directives. My way of dealing with the bureaucrats unfortunately was to become bureaucratic. I let my dislike of the scripted lesson plans get the best of me, so I just followed the plans exactly. If that was what the education bureaucracy wanted, that was what I would give them. The bureaucrats might like it, but it did no good for my students or me. The exemption is a great idea. The bureaucracy will be appeased, and my classroom will come alive again."

Paula had a similar idea for why Katy had not thought of that. "My guess was that the bureaucracy had defeated you, temporarily. You knew that you had to show evidence that content like the twenty vocabulary lists had been taught in your room. The simple way to satisfy a bureaucracy is to repeat its language back to it. So you used the provided lesson plans even though they had no art, music, or food. What they had was the most common and the most ordinary compliance with the curriculum mandate. For the rest of the curriculum, which was not accompanied with generic lesson plans, you got creative and did great work."

"Good analysis, Paula. With your support, I'll create some alternative lesson plans and ask for an exemption. You attend curriculum committee meetings, so please vote for my exemptions. Now one other concern: teaching really has changed in the thirteen years I've been a teacher. More students refuse to do homework. Fewer students read the types of books that are intellectually challenging. Students work more hours at their part-time jobs than ever. Athletes seem to practice or train for their sport for all twelve months of every year. Why is academic work such a low priority for more students than ever?

"And what am I supposed to do with a class of thirty-three students when one-third are scholars on their way to college for serious studies, one-third just want to pass and get out of here, and the other third miss class so much it is impossible to teach them? I don't remember having classes like that thirteen years ago. On my ordinary days, I guess I teach in ways that somehow keep all thirty-three students busy, or at least the twenty-five or so that showed up. On those days, the battle is just too exhausting to fight, but I just make myself do better the next day and try to be a great teacher again. This year has been erratic like that. What's your advice?"

Paula Marion needed to teach this teacher. What could she say or do to provide guidance and encouragement? Paula knew that much had changed in the past thirteen years. Ms. Vermont was right about the new reality that faced teachers now. Mrs. Marion also knew that students of today had many deep-down similarities with students of thirteen years ago or of a longer time in the past than thirteen years.

"Katy, I remember hearing my teachers thirty years ago say that teaching was not like it used to be. You are saying the same thing. Those teachers of mine were right. You are right. You are a good teacher. We've identified what has caused some days this year to be ordinary for you and your students. We have a plan to resolve that. Now, let's go further. Teaching thirteen years from now will be different than it is today. In thirteen years, we might look at this year as the good old days. Here's my point. Throughout the years you were a student and when I was a student, and throughout the years of our teaching careers, great teachers, including us, have known what great teachers have always known. What do you think great teachers know and have always known about the work of great teaching? Everything on your official evaluation is satisfactory, good, or great, but that evaluation form does not measure some of the essentials that great teachers know. So, what do great teachers, including Katy Vermont, know about great teaching?"

Katy had read many books about this topic when she earned her master's degree with an instruction and curriculum emphasis several years ago. Katy was also taking some online classes to expand her professional credentials to include school administration, and questions like this came up in some online discussions that Katy, her professors, and the other graduate school students shared.

"Here's my answer. Great teachers know that one size does not fit all. One type of instruction will not work for every student, so use the variety that works with this year's students. Great teachers know that, if they are excited about teaching, students are more likely to get excited about learning. They know that students will respond to meaningful challenges, not to pointless busy work. They know that students appreciate it when you care about them and take an interest in their interests, and great teachers know that if today's learning can connect with what already matters to students—like their career goals or their hobbies—the results are much better."

Paula was impressed. "Katy, when you do all of that, you are the great teacher you expect yourself to be and that you promised yourself thirteen years ago you would always be. Now, sign this form to confirm that we had this conference, please. But remember that this form cannot measure the heart and the soul that you put into your teaching when you are at your best. You expect more of yourself than any evaluation instrument can measure. You expect yourself to be a great teacher every day. Our profession needs more people like you. Our profession needs you, Katy."

As Katy left Paula's office, Paula glanced at her computer screen. There were thirteen new e-mails, there were three new electronic discipline referrals, and there was a clock reminding her to get out of the office and into the halls and supervise during the upcoming class break.

Paula also knew there was something her computer screen could not show. There was a great teacher, Katy Vermont, who had just reminded herself what great teachers know about the work of great teaching. Paula would love to be a student in Katy's next class. No doubt, the teaching and the learning would be great, greater, and greatest.

Those encouraging thoughts will be important to remember as we explore in the next chapter some details about what teachers cannot control and cannot manage. We also will explore coping skills for manageable realities. Yet, we must confront the unmanageable, the very difficult and frustrating realities, perhaps described as inclined to be resistant-to-management realities.

Chapter Five

What Teachers Cannot Control and Cannot Manage

- Experiences students have had before they come to your class
- The people students are related to, live with, and are influenced by
- The grades students have made thus far in their education
- The reading skills students have acquired or have not acquired so far
- The number of hours students are allowed to watch television at home
- The number of hours students are allowed to be on the computer at home
- Whether the student has a cell phone or not
- Whether the student has a car or not
- Whether the student has a part-time job or not
- How much time students invest in studying each day
- How much time students spend on extracurricular activities
- Responsibilities students have to their family, church, local community groups they participate in, and activities sponsored by those groups
- Hobbies that students have
- The attitude about school that students bring when they initially enter your classroom
- Friendships and romances that students are involved in
- How often students are absent from school
- Whether a student skips a class
- What students know about proper manners when they initially enter your classroom
- The work ethic students have developed
- The self-perception that each student has about how good a student he or she is
- Whether a student is in the habit of arriving at school on time and well prepared

- Whether a student is in the habit of completing homework on time and turning in homework on time
- How appreciative students and their families are for the effort teachers make for those students
- Whether families respond to information teachers provide about great work a student did, work a student did not do, great behavior by a student, or misbehavior by a student
- The discipline decisions made and actions taken by a school principal or assistant principal after a teacher has written a discipline referral
- The higher priorities that school administrators give to certain misbehaviors by students over other misbehaviors
- All of the other people who work at the school where you teach
- Who is in each of those other jobs at your school and how those people do their jobs
- The current laws in your state that govern education
- The current policies and regulations in your state and in your school district that govern education
- The increasing role of the U.S. national government in state and local education matters
- The promises politicians continually make about reforming education
- Announcements made over the school's public address system during class time
- School administrators and school counselors who need to see a student during class time
- Whether students had breakfast before the school day began
- Whether students get proper nutrition at home
- How much physical exercise students get outside of school
- How much sleep students get at home each night
- Whether or when there could be a failure of the electrical system at school
- Whether or when the computer system will not work at school
- Whether or when the copy machines will work at school
- Excuses students make for why they did not do their homework
- Excuses parents and guardians make for why their child did not do the homework, did not prepare for a test, or did not finish a project, even though it was assigned several weeks ago
- Media coverage about education
- The overall public perception of education
- When families move and a student enters your class during the school year
- When families move and a student leaves your class during the school year
- How much you are paid
- How much other people in education are paid
- When or if another teaching job at another school will become open

- Whether you will be selected for that other job that seems desirable to you
- When or if an assistant principal, a principal, or a school counselor job that you would like to move into becomes open
- Whether you will be selected for that principal, assistant principal, or school counselor job
- How efficient and updated the telephone system at school is
- The decision made about whether to cancel school due to bad weather
- Whether parents and guardians attend the school's annual open house
- Whether parents and guardians ever attend a class their child takes
- Whether parents and guardians attend athletic events, concerts, plays, or other extracurricular activities that their child participates in
- Whether teachers who also coach a sport work as hard on their teaching as they do on their coaching
- Whether the local newspaper pays more attention to high school sports than to high school scholars
- Who says what at faculty meetings
- Who attends faculty meetings
- Who is allowed to miss faculty meetings
- E-mails that are sent to everyone in the school
- The potentially endless e-mail chain that continues as people respond to the first e-mail and, for unknown reasons, copy everyone in the school
- Medical conditions with which students are managing and coping and that can become a classroom emergency
- Disabilities that students are managing, coping with, and hopefully, over-coming
- Students who are court involved, have been convicted, have been in juvenile jail, who are repeat offenders, and who are in school now
- Students whose family has had a very contentious divorce with lingering animosities and complicated parental or guardian arrangements
- Very precise court orders about which adult or adults may see a student or pick up a student
- Equally precise court orders about which adult or adults may not see a student or pick up a student
- The increasing number of students being reared by a grandparent or by grandparents
- Students who are in school and are pregnant
- Students who commit crimes at school or elsewhere
- Students who use drugs, including alcohol, at school or elsewhere
- Students who intend to drop out of school as soon as they are allowed to drop out legally
- Students whose family members do not value education
- Students who have never met their father
- Students whose mothers are in jail

- Students who are capable of doing more work and more advanced work than any class or any program the school offers
- The next time a student will violate rules and pull the fire alarm at the school
- The next time someone phones in a bomb threat
- The next time a student nominates his or her teacher for an award

Now, please take a few minutes and add to the above list of those realities that teachers cannot control and cannot manage.

1.

2.

3.

4.

5.

6.

7.

8.

9.

10.

Given these many facts, realities, circumstances, and challenges that teachers cannot control and cannot manage, what's a teacher to do?

Teachers can control and can manage their *responses* to these facts, realities, circumstances, and challenges. To analyze the impact of these responses, the work experiences of two middle school teachers will serve as examples.

Anne Ridgeway's family knew she had a gift for art when she was five years old. When Anne and her friends would play, Anne was always the source of creativity. She invented new games. She created imaginary adventures and invited her friends to join her in designing a fantasy world. Then Anne would draw what that fantasy world looked like. Her family knew that these sketches were a preview of magnificent art to come as Anne grew in knowledge of art.

Anne's family took her to art museums during her elementary school and middle school years. When the family traveled anywhere for any reason, they would include visits to art studios, art exhibitions, college or university art displays, and art fairs, and Anne would absorb the wonder, beauty, power, and joy of art.

Anne's high school art teacher realized how exceptional Anne's art talent was. She introduced Anne to new art studio possibilities through which Anne could display her art and sell her art. This teacher also guided Anne to college scholarship possibilities that led to Anne attending a university known internationally for its premier art program.

At the end of her sophomore year in college Anne declared her major. She chose art, of course, and because years ago art had chosen Anne, it was recognized as a perfect match. Anne also applied for and was accepted to the university's college of education teacher preparation program. Anne thought she would like to be a private art teacher, have her own art studio, create art, and teach students how to create art.

During her junior year of college, Anne's teaching methods class required her to visit a middle school for ten hours and a high school for ten hours. The middle school visits changed Anne's thoughts about teaching.

The middle school had a new principal who was determined to energize the school, which for years had underachieved. Part of the energizing plan was for the building itself to look like a place that was uniquely designed for and decorated by middle school students. Student-created artwork was to fill the school. The principal's goal was for every wall in the building to be the opposite of school-wall beige, which seemed to be everywhere. No walls of the classrooms, hallways, cafeteria, gym, locker rooms, office area, library, or stairwells were to be left in school-wall beige.

Anne volunteered to help with this paint-the-school project. Her ten hours of required observation time expanded to include fifty more hours of working with students and teachers to paint the school. The interaction with students, the joy of seeing students create art throughout their school, and the energy and enthusiasm that filled the school as art was created, admired, and appreciated touched Anne's heart, soul, and mind. She began thinking that teaching art to curious, creative, lively, unpredictable, and eager middle school students could be a good career choice. She could teach middle school, teach private art lessons, participate in summer art events, and fulfill all of her art dreams.

When Anne graduated from college, she was in the midst of applying to many school districts for an art teaching job. The formal application process had begun in February of her senior year in college, but the informal process had begun during her senior year's first semester, when she was a student teacher for two good months at a high school and for two fantastic months at the same middle school where she had helped with the total school art adventure during her junior year.

Finally, as the college years were ending, there were three job interviews. Anne had been impatient and anxious in March and April, but schools apparently needed time to sort out personnel matters for the next school year. In May, Anne heard from three principals, and she had three interviews. She had deeply hoped for an opportunity to teach at her adopted middle school, but there was no opening there. Anne decided she would take what she had done and learned there to another school in hopes of creating another total school art immersion project.

Anne had one job offer after those three interviews. She quickly accepted this middle school art teaching position. The other two interviews had been at high schools, and Anne thought she had done well in each interview, so she wondered why one middle school said yes as two high schools said no. She was thrilled and thankful to have her middle school art teaching job, but the part of her that always seeks to know more led her to talk with one of her college professors to get some perspective and understanding.

"Anne, I can tell you what I have seen through the years and what can happen in situations like this. High schools sometimes have many coaching jobs that need to be filled. You are a gifted artist, and you will be an outstanding art teacher. You are not a sports coach. So, maybe those high schools each used their art vacancy to also fill a coaching vacancy. They might have chosen someone to teach because they also knew the person could coach, or maybe they chose a graduate of the high school."

Anne asked, "Would they select someone who was not the best art teacher so they could get someone who can coach or get someone they knew years ago?"

The professor was blunt. "Yes. That can happen. It may not be admitted, but it happens. You and I cannot control that. We can't control when a school selects a person for a job because they knew them from their student teaching or from substitute teaching or from some other association. We cannot control when a school has to factor in some need for diversity on the faculty. We can't control when a high school sees someone as a middle school person only or a middle school sees someone as a high school person only. What you can control is everything you will provide for your middle school students. This can be a dream-come-true job for you."

Anne agreed. "You are right. I can't wait. Thanks for your help during college and now. I'll keep in touch."

At a nearby college, Meredith Cleveland was graduating with a double major in journalism and English. She was interested in the advertising business, but friends had told her that jobs in advertising can come and go with ups and downs in the economy. Meredith was advised to earn certification to teach English so she would have, as some people always said, "something to fall back on." Falling back into a job seemed strange to Meredith, but she knew what people meant about job security. Meredith graduated from college in the same month that Anne did. They had never met, but that would change soon.

Meredith sent forty-seven applications to various advertising agencies, marketing companies, large corporations, public relations firms, nonprofit organizations, and political campaigns. The results of this six-month process was that, when she graduated from college, she had received twenty-three replies of "nothing is available," twenty-two no replies at all, and two job interviews that went nowhere. It was difficult to compete in a tight job market with people who had ten, twenty, or more years of experience.

Meredith spent part of May and much of June applying for English teaching jobs in five school districts in the region close to her college, which was in her hometown. She applied online. She completed paper applications. She got letters of recommendations. She personally took her resume to eighteen schools. She called those eighteen schools to follow up.

Meredith took her resume to a nineteenth school, Jefferson Middle School, the school where Anne Ridgeway had been hired a few weeks earlier. The principal was standing at the front counter in the office when Meredith walked in. The principal, Kim Raymond, spoke with Meredith and mentioned that, just the day before, an English teacher at the school had been selected to become the new assistant principal for Jefferson Middle School. Meredith tried to be polite and measured, but her eagerness for and desperation for a job exploded into a very sincere "I'd love to teach here. I'd love to interview for that job. My application is up to date. You have my resume and my phone number."

Ms. Raymond was impressed with Meredith's enthusiasm. "Well, Meredith, we'll have an interviewing committee set up today or tomorrow. If that committee decides to include you in the interviews, you'll hear from us next week. Thank you for stopping by today."

The next few days passed with painful slowness for Meredith. Each time the phone ran, she jumped. Finally, the ultimate call came. Yes, she would be delighted to interview for the seventh-grade English teaching job at Jefferson Middle School. Yes, she would be there at nine on Friday morning.

The interview went well. The committee was impressed with Meredith's idea of creating an elective journalism class that would organize a morning television broadcast of the school announcements, publish an online school newspaper, greatly expand the capabilities of the school's website, and create the school's first video yearbook.

It was slightly awkward when Meredith was asked if teaching middle school English was her number-one job preference or if she saw herself more as a high school teacher where there could be more journalism classes. Meredith diplomatically replied that building a journalism class and program at

Jefferson Middle School really interested her. What she did not say was that being employed was her greatest interest. She figured that everyone on the committee understood that recent college graduates were eager to get their first job.

Meredith was selected for the job, although two of the committee members thought that other candidates who were experienced teachers deserved to be considered more seriously. Meredith's recent college experiences with up-to-the-minute technology mastery were a clear advantage for her. Kim Raymond envisioned a paperless school where everything was done online or with other electronic methods. What Meredith was proposing for the journalism class could become a model for technology use in every classroom.

Jefferson Middle School had a one-day orientation program for new teachers in mid-August before the students returned to school on August 23. There were six new teachers at the school, although four of them did have some teaching experience as substitute teachers. Anne and Meredith were the two people who were absolutely new to teaching.

It was during the new teacher orientation meeting that Anne and Meredith got acquainted. During lunch, they talked about their college experiences, about the lengthy search for a teaching job, and about the classes they would be teaching.

Anne's ideas for art and Meredith's ideas for video school news broadcasts, an online school newspaper, and a video yearbook had many similarities. They began to think of ways to involve art students in the journalism class and journalism students in art classes. The other teachers who were new to Jefferson Middle School had their conversations during part of lunch, but as Anne and Meredith got more excited about their symbiotic ideas, everyone joined in the discussion. The excitement grew. The plans got more dramatic and creative. There would be no limits to what could be accomplished when capable people listened to each other, traded ideas, created plans together, and dreamed bold dreams.

Then the school year began. The first week of school can be consumed with procedures and schedule changes, with forms to fill out and records to update, with rules to learn and with questions to answer. New students need to learn their way throughout the building. New teachers need to learn their way throughout their duties.

Finally, by the third day of school, a regular routine was established. The forms were filled out, and the rules were learned. Some schedules would still be changed. Some students would still have trouble finding the right classroom or getting their locker to unlock. Some new teacher would wonder if every day would be as exhausting as days one and two were.

Anne and Meredith saw each other only for a quick moment on the first and second days of school, but they agreed to get together in Anne's classroom after school on Friday. Meredith did not have a classroom. The school was built for 675 students, but enrollment for this year had been projected to be 752, and on the third day of school, there were 758 students in attendance with 39 absences, so enrollment was going to be close to 800. Too many students and not enough classrooms meant that some teachers had to float from classroom to classroom during the school day. Art was a class that never floated, due to all of the art supplies, materials, and equipment that had to stay in one place. Seventh-grade English could float, so Meredith floated.

Meredith arrived in Anne's classroom about 3:55 on the third day of school, a few minutes following her completion of after-school bus supervision. Anne had early-morning cafeteria duty this week. Meredith closed the door and began a vibrant monologue.

"I can't believe this place. I can't believe these students. Forget everything we said about art and journalism working together. I would never put these students on a live television broadcast even just within the school. I would not trust them with an online school newspaper or any other school newspaper. Forget the video yearbook. They would destroy the cameras and other equipment. What's wrong with these students? They yell. They fight. They talk all the time. Their language in the halls is evil and crude. Their manners don't exist. They complain about everything we do in class. They play with their cell phones. I sound old, but why do they need a cell phone. My seventh graders seem to need a babysitter or a parole officer or some punishment like people in the colonies or the middle ages used. Is it any better for you?"

Actually, the first three days of school had gone well for Anne and her six classes of art students. Everything Anne and the students had done involved art. When she checked attendance in each class on the first day of school, Anne had each student say his or her name and favorite color. Then the students got into groups by the color they chose and learned each other's names. Then they told the entire class what was so good about their color. On the second day of school, Anne used shapes—triangle, arc, rectangle, circle, cylinder, octagon, and others—for the students to select. On the third day of school, Anne replaced color and shape with famous works of art, which she had big posters of around the room. Each student selected his or her favorite artwork and stood by it, and the learning activity continued.

"It's been better than I expected. I've used a lot of activities, a lot of variety, some movement, and everyone has been involved. A few students were still in summer vacation attitude, but that will pass. They have a homework assignment for Monday, and I think it will go well."

Meredith was in the same school building but having a very different experience. "Homework. I can't get them to do schoolwork at school. Why do I have to make them work or motivate them to work or entice them to work? It's their job to be a student. I talked to one of the school counselors yesterday. She told me that a lot of these students have problems at home.

She said that many of them forget what they learned last year during summer vacation. She said that they have weak reading skills and weak math skills. How did they get to the seventh grade? Who passed them each year to the next grade if they can't read well or do math well?"

Anne did not have answers to all of those questions. She did have an idea. "Here are the lesson plans I have for my classes for next week. I made some changes in these plans based on what I picked up from the students in class. The other thing I did was talk to some of the sixth- and seventh-grade teachers yesterday. I have all of the grades. You have only seventh graders, so you could talk to the sixth-grade teachers and find out from them what worked in sixth-grade English classes last year. They could also tell you what didn't work. I teach sixth, seventh, and eighth grades. What I learned from some sixth- and seventh-grade teachers about this school and these students helps me. I think my original lesson plans were good, but if they aren't good for my students right now, then they had to change."

Meredith had different ideas. "I think the students need to change. They need to follow rules and instructions. They need to work. They need to leave their problems and their excuses behind. They'll never be ready for high school if they don't get serious about something. I'll show them that they have to get serious about seventh-grade English. If they insist on making this miserable for me, I'll make it more miserable for them. The reading assignment they have for next week should show them what they are up against."

Anne's last idea was that she and Meredith should visit again at the end of the second week of school to keep sharing experiences and ideas. Meredith agreed, and after school on Friday of the second week, they met in Anne's room.

"Well, out of my 142 students, 87 made an F on the reading assignment. Forty-three made a D, and ten made a C. There were two B grades, and no student made an A grade."

"Meredith, what was the reading assignment that the students had?"

"Anne, I brought a copy for you. There were two short stories to read. One was about the experience of an American soldier in World War II. The other was about the experience of an American astronaut in the 1960s. There were questions so the students could compare and contrast the stories. Most students turned in nothing. Some turned in paragraphs they printed from the Internet that had almost nothing to do with the assignment. A few students copied each other's work word for word. So, no more assignments like that. I heard another teacher talking about how lazy his eighth-grade English students are. He gives them a packet of worksheets to do each day. Everyone is quiet, and everyone knows the routine. He said he got the idea from a sixth-grade teacher who said it was the only way to control the students. So, we did the same thing yesterday. It was great. The students knew what to do. Some of them had that sixth-grade teacher last year, and they knew the routine from her class."

Anne was curious about the results. "How did the students do? Did they finish the worksheets?"

"Almost all of them did. A few talked or went to sleep. I just gave them an extra worksheet each time they talked or slept. I think the system can work. And the best part is the English teachers have boxes and files of worksheets I can use. I'm going to stay late today and make copies of the worksheets I'll use with my classes for the next month. If this is the only way to control these students, we'll do worksheets forever. How was the week for you?"

"It was good. I began a project with each grade level on Monday, and by Friday the room was filled with all of these great works of art. With sixth graders, they were to use newspapers, boxes, and aluminum foil to make sculpture. Seventh graders used all kinds of pieces of fabrics to make a type of quilt. Eighth graders made an illustrated map that would give new students or visitors a walking tour of the school building. Students could work individually or in small groups. All of the projects were presented in class on Friday, and we filmed those presentations so we can make a video about the work each class did. On Monday, we will analyze the process that was used from the artistic concept students had through the project they completed. Then we'll watch a short video of an interview I did with a great artist who taught a college class I took. I called her a few days ago, and we did this great webcam interview. We'll evaluate what the students did in their process of making art and see how similar it is to what that great artist did. Then everyone will write an analysis of the similarities or differences."

Meredith said, "Anne, that sounds risky. It sounds like a lot of work for you. I would never be able to give my students the freedom to create a project. My students have shown me that they need a very strict structure and a very rigid routine. Well, I've got thousands of copies to make. Nobody stays to work after school on Friday, so I should have both copy machines to myself. Have a good weekend, Anne."

"You, too, Meredith," Anne said as she looked around her art room and proudly celebrated with a smile. Her students were becoming artists. Control of her students was not done by worksheets. The adventurous process of learning about art in ways that apply the inherent curiosity and energy of middle school students provided its own structure without seeming to be structured. Anne knew she could not control the ability and the experiences that the students brought to class with them, but she could control how the students acquired new abilities and were given new experiences designed just for them.

The reader is asked to reflect on the case study about Anne and Meredith. What workplace realities were they facing? What could they control at school, and what could they not control at school? Which approach, Anne's or Meredith's, makes more sense, given the realities of their school and of their classes? Is there some merit in both approaches? What results will Anne and her students likely get? What results are likely for Meredith and her students? What would you do if you were in Anne's job or in Meredith's job?

The school board had made the decision. It was now a policy. Every teacher in the school district would submit detailed lesson plans in writing or via electronic communication every Friday for the upcoming week. Each school would design the lesson plan format that had to be used at the school. The principal or an assistant principal would receive the lesson plans by noon on Friday. If Friday was scheduled as a day when school was not in session, the last school day of the week would be the due day for lesson plans.

The school principal or the assistant principal would read each lesson plan and provide some reply to each teacher, probably via electronic communication, before the school day began on Monday. If school was not scheduled to be in session on Monday, the administrator's reply was to be received by all teachers before school began on the first school day of the week.

The faculty meeting at Jefferson Middle School had a limited agenda, so after some announcements and reports, Principal Kim Raymond distributed copies of the school board's new policy about lesson plans. The policy was to be implemented by October 1, so there was no time to spare in the few weeks between this faculty meeting and the October 1 start date. The transcript of the discussion that followed Kim's presentation of everything she knew about the policy is below:

Nick Mitchell: It's a policy, so we have to follow it, but isn't this just one more example of micromanagement? Does the school board really have the legal authority to dictate this? Can they mandate this legally? Don't schools have some authority on issues like this? I'll do what the policy requires, of course. I'm not going to be defiant. But as I comply with the policy, I'll express my thought that the school board continues to limit what we can do. Should I spend my time creating great lessons and doing great teaching, or should I spend my time getting some forms filled out by noon on each Friday?

Jane Irvine: So each school is supposed to design its lesson plan format to use, right? That's a problem. There are forty or fifty teachers here. We teach sixth, seventh, and eighth graders. We teach lots of different subjects. How can one lesson plan format work for every subject and every grade? Isn't this just going to force us into a more cookie-cutter approach where we just do less and less innovative teaching because lesson plan forms usually don't have any way to appreciate creativity or innovation? Doesn't this just invite more "read the chapter, answer the questions, finish the worksheet" type of lesson plans because that's what a form can measure?

Celeste Cooper: The school year just started. We are getting to know our students, and we are finding out what works and maybe what doesn't work. We have tons of stuff to do in these early weeks of the school year. What is the school board thinking? Was this their idea, or did the state department of education tell every school board to do something like this? Did the officials in our school district recommend this to the school board? Did somebody go to some national conference and hear a presentation about mandatory lesson plans as the way to reform schools, so now everyone has to do this? Just let me teach. Find some way to stop these mandates from the higher-ups, and just let me teach.

Tasha Moyer: We'll never win this battle. We are employees of the school district. The school board is the highest authority in the school district. They made the policy, and we have to follow it. At least we can create a lesson form for our school. The school board is telling us what to do, but they are not telling us exactly how to do it.

Anne Ridgeway: That's a great point. We do have some freedom in this. The lesson plan format we use is what we create. So let's take advantage of that freedom to make the lesson plan format what we want it to be.

Meredith Cleveland: I'm new to teaching, so I don't know that much about lesson plan formats. What I do know is that with all of the problems some students bring with them to school, it seems to me that the school board could spend their time on more important things. Is there any way we can help them understand what the real problems are so they don't think that their policy on lesson plans will solve everything?

Shawn Bishop: Let's move on. The policy is a fact. We have to do this. I suggest that we create the most concise lesson plan form possible. Let's comply, but let's make it take the least amount of time we can. It's one more chore for us. A great lesson takes more time and thought than any form can contain. We'll teach well; we always do, not because of some lesson plan mandate or format, but because we expect ourselves to do professional work. Kim, what needs to happen next so we can move on?

Kim Raymond: We need a group of teachers to design a proposed lesson plan format. It would be great to get at least one teacher from each grade level and at least one elective teacher. Others are welcome. Anyone who would like to serve on that committee can meet with me right after we finish our faculty meeting. We'll get a recommendation together for the entire faculty to review and comment on, and then we can reach final agreement in a week or two on our lesson plan format. Thank you for your attention and participation today. Have a good evening.

What could teachers and administrators not control about the school board policy? What was the policy intended to achieve? What is the school board attempting to control? Would the school board see its action as one of control, or would they see their action as having other motives and intentions? What perceptions would teachers usually have about policies such as the lesson plan policy? What perceptions would principals and assistant principals usually have about policies such as the lesson plan policy? When should a teacher express concern about or opposition to a policy, and when should a policy just be accepted as part of the reality of teaching?

Is Anne dreaming or is she realistic when she suggests that there could be benefits and advantages for the school and for teachers if people will contribute ideas to help design a lesson plan format that will enhance instruction, will be beneficial for students, and could be useful for teachers? Was Meredith's concern realistic, cynical, or based in frustration that the school reality was more severe than she expected?

Toward the end of the first semester, Anne and Meredith met for their weekly discussion on a December Friday after school. Anne's students continued to respond well to creative, interesting, active learning experiences and to the writing analysis that was part of each experience. Meredith's students were complying with the daily routine of worksheets with fewer discipline problems because their teachers had always controlled them with worksheets. The student knew the routine, and it was really easy to get by.

Today, Meredith had a question for Anne. "Do you notice that some teachers get here about one minute before school starts and they leave about one minute after school dismisses? How do they get away with that? And some teachers are scheduled for more weeks of early morning duty or after-school duty than other teachers. Do those people who arrive late and leave early ever have the supervisor duties the rest of us have?"

Anne had not noticed much of that. "I never really noticed much about when people arrive or leave. I do hear interesting comments now and then, but I don't pay any attention. I know when I get here and when I leave. It takes time to prepare for classes each morning and to finish everything that came up during the day. Some parts of teaching can be done only before or after school. I put in the hours it takes to do the work well."

Meredith was still somewhat annoyed. "Yeah, I put in the time it takes to do my work the way it needs to be done. I just don't see how some people get away with doing so little, at least in terms of the hours they are here. And one more thing. Are you getting e-mails from parents asking you to let a student take a test over or turn in extra credit or do something else to improve their grade? I tell them that everyone has the same chance to make a good grade, but no exceptions will be made. Late work is a zero grade. I give no extra credit. Why would parents ask for second chances? Don't they want their child to be responsible?"

"Well, they may think they are doing the child a favor, but it can backfire if the student thinks a parent or guardian can always get them out of academic trouble or other trouble. I gave every student a copy of the classroom rules and procedures. I gave everyone an extra copy to take home. I e-mailed a copy to every family we have an e-mail address for. I posted the same information on my Web page. When I get an e-mail like the ones you mentioned, I reply with a copy of my classroom rules and procedures, plus I copy the principal on my e-mail reply in case she gets a call or an e-mail about it."

Meredith was ready to go make copies of worksheets for the next week. Anne was going to stay and work some on her lesson plans for next week. She had sent them electronically to Mrs. Raymond on Thursday and had received some very helpful suggestions early on Friday morning.

Meredith had turned in her lesson plans by noon on Friday. She expected very little commentary on her lesson plans because they were almost identical week to week. She complied with the lesson plan schedule. She followed the format. She added more when she was told to add more, and she occasionally tried some teaching method other than worksheets. Those other methods rarely worked, but she could say she had tried. She could not control the fact that her students seemed to do best with packets of worksheets.

Anne taught some of the same students. Anne never used packets of worksheets. Her students seemed to do best with a variety of vibrant, creative, challenging activities. How could the same students thrive in Anne's creative, yet orderly, classroom when it seemed to require the rigid routine of worksheets and more worksheets as discipline action in another class? Anne manages instruction differently than Meredith manages instruction. What does that reality reveal about what teachers cannot control and cannot manage contrasted with what teachers can control and can manage?

Toward the end of the school year, Kim Raymond will complete her final evaluations of all teachers. Kim will recommend to the school district whether teachers should be hired for another year or not hired for another year. Because Anne and Meredith are first-year teachers, they are several years away from earning tenure or any similar form of a continuing contract. The recommendations Kim will make are based on the facts of each teacher's work performance.

Is Kim's recommendation something that a teacher can control and can manage? Is Kim's recommendation something that a teacher cannot control and cannot manage?

Based on what is known about Anne and Meredith, what words might Kim Raymond use to evaluate the work done by each of these teachers during their first year of teaching? What recommendation would you expect Kim to make about Anne? What recommendation would you expect Kim to make about Meredith?

The long list at the start of this chapter indicated that there are many realities about school that teachers cannot control and cannot manage. How teachers respond to those realities varies from person to person. One variable could be how much a teacher is inspired by, motivated by, dedicated to, and persistent about the dream of teaching. Teachers cannot control and cannot manage many realities they are faced with, but how they face those realities is part of what teachers can control and can manage. Some teachers face the dream and bring reality with them. Other teachers face reality and permit the dream to fade. The next chapter provides details about what teachers can control and what teachers can manage.

Chapter Six

What Teachers Can Control and Can Manage

Joseph Chrisman teaches high school social studies classes to ninth graders and to twelfth graders. He has taught for eighteen years at the same school. With that much seniority at Jackson High School, he could select any classes he would prefer to teach.

Mr. Chrisman teaches two classes of ninth-grade civics because the high school freshman failure rate is a local problem and a national concern. Mr. Chrisman's ninth graders do not fail. Some of Joe's freshmen struggle, complain, rebel, get in trouble, act silly, make excuses, and push the limits, but Joe knows what to do. He has seen everything a mischievous high school freshman can do, and he is one step ahead of each year's ninth graders who mistakenly think that they invented the same schemes that Mr. Chrisman has outsmarted for eighteen years.

Joe Chrisman also teaches four classes of political science to seniors. A few high school juniors take this class, but it is designed to be a culminating high school class that applies the accumulated knowledge of students who have taken ninth-grade civics, tenth-grade world history, and eleventh-grade U.S. history. The students in Mr. Chrisman's political science class know they are being taught a class that has academic content and work demands equal to a college class. There are many books to read, much research to do, and no extra credit; no late work is accepted, and the classroom is a combination of no-nonsense, high intellectual achievement, and much cordial interaction. The students learn that Mr. Chrisman demands their total commitment to class and that Mr. Chrisman gives the students his total commitment.

Every year, a few uninformed students innocently sign up for and get scheduled into the political science class expecting an easy credit. What were they thinking? Within one or two days after the beginning of school, these few students beg their school counselor to change their schedule. "It's too much work. We have a test on the third day of class. We have a book to read for next week. We have a research project due in two weeks."

The students who stay in the class learn political science thoroughly. Those students also learn more than they realized they could ever know about serious, scholarly, academic study. They have had great classes taught by great teachers, but by design Mr. Chrisman and the teachers of English classes and math classes have worked together to include in the political science class two major research papers, one of which must include very sophisticated analysis of data related to political campaigns or to public policy.

This interdisciplinary approach takes much time, effort, and coordination by Mr. Chrisman, who gets essential advice from his English and math teaching colleagues. This approach also gives the political science students a learning, working, and scholarly experience that is more than preparation for college; rather, it is designed to equal a college experience.

Joe Chrisman is not required to make his political science class a college-level experience. Joe could very easily reduce the quality of and the quantity of the work that he requires students to do. Joe would get paid no more money and no less money if he simplified the class, relied on one textbook, used only the classroom instructional materials provided by the textbook publisher, used only tests a machine can grade, and showed a long video at least once per week. Joe has set a much higher standard for himself than any employment contract or job description in his profession could establish. Joe can control and manage the quality of the learning experience that his students have. Joe insists on the best possible learning experience for his students, which also means that Joe gives himself the best possible teaching experience.

Joe noticed a few years ago that high school students were taking math and science classes that an earlier generation waited to take in college. If the math curriculum and the science curriculum in high school could be advanced, and if high school students could succeed in those otherwise college classes, then the social studies curriculum could also advance to the college level. Joe knew that his high school properly provided many options for and much academic support for students who struggled in school or who were at risk of dropping out of school. As a matter of fairness, Joe Chrisman decided to make sure that the most capable students were given the academic challenges they deserved while also welcoming students who were willing to work hard and develop their intellectual capabilities.

As Joe Chrisman takes us on a tour of a day in his life as a high school teacher, the reader is asked to pay particular attention to the events, activities, circumstances, situations, and interactions Joe can control or manage and those Joe cannot control or manage. Notice if there are opportunities Joe is missing where he could exert more control. Notice if there are any situations where Joe tries to manage something beyond his influence.

A DAY IN THE LIFE OF JOE CHRISMAN, TEACHER

A favorite part of each day for me is the early morning. My wife and our children like to sleep later, but I get up about 5:00 each morning. I take time to read a little, and I use our treadmill to get thirty minutes of exercise. I'm cleaned up, dressed, and ready for the day as everyone else is waking up about 6:15 or 6:30.

Our family has breakfast together every weekday morning at 6:45. We begin with a prayer. We read a Bible verse together. We confirm our plans for the day and for the upcoming days. Our son is sixteen, and our daughter is fourteen. David is a high school junior, and Andrea is a high school freshman. They both do very well in school, and they are active in several school activities. David is getting close to reaching his goal of starting on the soccer team. Andrea is very excited about being in the marching band. I teach at Jackson High School, but our children attend the other high school in our county. You can imagine what it is like when Jackson High School competes with Burlington Memorial High School.

By 7:15 each morning, I am on my way to school. My wife, Lauren, manages information technology for a local hospital. The hospital is close to Burlington Memorial High School, so Lauren takes David and Andrea to school. They ride the bus home after school unless they stay for practices, and then we pick them up or we have a carpool with other families.

By 7:30 most mornings, I am in my classroom. I turn on the computer. If I have to make any copies, I go to the faculty workroom and hope both copy machines are working, hope there is enough paper for the copies I need, hope my monthly quota of copies is not near the limit, and hope there is no line for making copies.

On this day, I was at school by 7:25 because some students will arrive at 7:30 to take makeup tests, since their science class had a field trip yesterday when we had a major political science test. I had made all the copies of everything for today when I stayed a little longer than usual yesterday. The makeup tests add to my workload, but there is not much I can do about it.

The three seniors who had to make up the test are on time. They know that makeup time is Tuesday morning from 7:30 to 8:25 with no earlier start and no time extension. When we have tests in class, I allocate no more than fifty-five minutes of a class block of ninety minutes, so the makeup time equals the maximum time for a test on the regular in-class schedule.

While the three students take their tests, I have more than enough to do. It's like this every day. That's why I arrive one hour before the first block class starts at 8:30 each morning. If I arrived at 7:00 or 6:45, I would use that extra time, but my family and I have a routine of time together each morning and that will not change, plus I need that quiet time and exercise early in the morning at home.

I do notice the teachers who arrive about 8:20 or so. It's not my job to tell them when to get here, but I can't imagine giving yourself only ten minutes between when you arrive and when your first class starts. Different people have different ideas about how to do this job.

Things like that go on my someday list. Someday, when I'm a high school assistant principal or principal, we will have a very clear and very precisely enforced policy about the latest allowable arrival time at school and earliest allowable exit time after school. When Andrea graduates from high school, our family schedule will change, and I intend to get into school administration then. My someday list has been growing during my teaching career. A few items on it got marked off as our school improvement committee responded to my ideas or to similar ideas from other people. Still, it's a long list. It will take five or ten years to get everything on my someday list finished whenever I do become a school administrator.

While the students were taking their makeup test, I got some computer work done. E-mail saves time and consumes time. There were six e-mails that needed replies. I updated the Web page that shows students and their families what we are doing in classes. I keep it updated so they can always see the schedule of reading, tests, quizzes, projects, and everything else for the next two weeks.

There were some quizzes that my ninth-grade classes took yesterday. I graded them after school yesterday and put those grades in the computer this morning. Our school has a policy that papers of any type—homework, tests, quizzes, or projects—have to be graded and returned to students within two weeks. The policy says the grade must be in the computer before the paper is returned to the students. I would never make students wait for two weeks. If we have a quiz on Monday, the block schedule says that class will meet again on Wednesday and Friday of that week. I get the papers back no later than the second time a class meets after the paper was due or the test was taken. If papers are returned fast, the work is still fresh in the students' minds and my comments on their work mean more. Add that schedule of returning papers to my someday list.

Speaking of grading papers, that eats up a lot of time. I know some teachers who never give any homework. Those same teachers give quizzes and tests that are the multiple-choice type machines can grade. They never give essay questions on their tests because it takes so long to grade the essays. I keep suggesting we set up a policy to require writing in every class, but it gets rejected for vague reasons like "We have to let each person do what works best for their class." Show me the class whose no homework and nothing but machine-graded multiple-choice tests are what works best.

Two of the seniors had finished the makeup test by 8:15, and the third student was finished by 8:20. Some of my first block students were ready to come in at 8:20, but they know on Tuesdays to wait until 8:25 if anyone is still working on a makeup test. I started, but did not quite finish, a college letter of recommendation for a brilliant senior. I taught her when she was in ninth grade, and she is taking political science now. In the letter, I sincerely recommended that the college admissions officer call the student immediately and say she is accepted for admission. She is polite, conscientious, and brilliant; she works hard, is involved in school activities and community service, has had perfect attendance in high school, and is taking the most demanding class schedule a high school senior can take.

Those college letters of recommendation take a lot of time to write. I have heard a few teachers say they limit the number of letters of recommendation they will write in any one year. A teacher said a few days ago that ten letters per year was her limit for college letters, scholarship letters, letters to help a student get a job, or any other letter. The first ten students who ask for a letter get a letter. The teacher tells any other student they will have to get someone else to write their letter.

I just disagree with that limit. To be honest, that limit offends me. I wonder if ten students ask that teacher for a letter. With her attitude about letters, students probably rarely ask her to write a letter for them or do anything else for them. We should have a policy that says, when a student asks for a letter, write it. Sure, it takes time. Sure, some teachers get asked more than others. The students know which teachers care the most about them.

Here's something else I do. When a student asks me to write a letter to help them get a job, I'll do that if there is any possible way I can honestly recommend them for employment. If the student causes trouble and makes bad grades, I'll tell them to get a teacher whose class they behave better in and get a better grade in to write their letter. There are very few times I have had to do that, but each time the student knew I was being honest and knew that some work needed to be done to improve things in class.

For all of the other students whom I can enthusiastically endorse for a job, I write the best possible letter. That's not all. I call the potential employers, I e-mail the letter and a short note, or I go to the business and talk to the manager. It's just a promise I made myself of something extra that I would do for my students. They are always amazed. "Mr. Chrisman, I got the job. Those people could not believe that you actually went there to tell them to hire me. They said that never happens." It can happen, and the student always increases the effort in our class when it does happen, so everyone wins.

At 8:20, our school has a bell that sends the ten-minute warning to everyone. Be in class no later than ten minutes after the 8:20 bell. I had caught up on e-mail replies, but during the thirty minutes of 7:50 a.m. to 8:20 a.m., nine more e-mails arrived. One was from a retired teacher I had worked with. She was applying to be a substitute teacher and needed a letter of recommendation. Another e-mail was from our school district's human resources office requesting that I complete the electronic letter of recommendation form for that retired teacher. The electronic process does eliminate paper and does simplify the correspondence. It still takes time, but someday I'll need people to write letters for me, so I'll treat them now the way I hope they will treat me later.

Most of the other e-mails were just telling people about meetings to attend, an online professional development program every teacher and staff member has to complete, and a notice to delay taking attendance due to some traffic problems near the school. The online professional development is about time management. It's hard to resist the thought that I could manage my time better if I did not have to spend an hour after school one day completing the online animated stories and multiple-choice questions about time management.

At 8:25, the five-minute warning bell rings loudly. Students know they should be in their seat in the first-period classroom by the time the next bell rings at 8:30 or they can be marked tardy. Some teachers tell students they just need to be in the classroom. There is not a specific policy, so I tell students to be in their seat when the bell rings, but I realize that the enrollment in this school is much more than the building was designed for. When the 8:30 bell rings, I stand at the door and any of my students whom I see in the hall are allowed to come in. Then I close the door, and anyone who arrives after that must have an admit-to-class form from the attendance office. It is quite rare that any of my students are late to first-period class. I'd like to think it is because of our mutual trust and mutual respect. Another factor just might be that, when a student is officially tardy to first-period class, I e-mail their parent or guardian later that day. The problem almost never happens a second time for any student.

At 8:29, the phone rang and a teacher told me that one of my first block students had just finished a makeup test in calculus class. The student would be about one minute late to class. At 8:30, the bell rang, and despite crowded hallways moments earlier and despite traffic problems in the school's neighborhood, all of my students, except the one I had a call about, were in their seats. I should give a test because no student would have to make up the test, but we have other plans for the day.

The day begins with the Pledge of Allegiance. A student leads this as part of the 8:30 a.m. televised announcements. Then we watch and listen to the announcements. On a good day, the announcements take only about three minutes. On other days, the announcements go on to last four, five, or six minutes. Each minute of the announcements is a minute I am not teaching. I insist that everyone listen to the announcements because that is polite and because something is said on the announcements each day that someone in the class needs to know. I cannot control the length of the announcements, but I can manage how well my students listen during that time.

Finally, at 8:35 a.m., since all of my students are here, I have entered our attendance in the computer, and with the five-minute announcement broadcast over, the twenty-eight young scholars in the classroom and I are ready to explore, analyze, and understand the complexities of political science. The short news clip from last night's network news archives that I was going to use is not available because, at 8:36, the Internet at our school went down. We move on to distribute the copies of a twentieth-century presidential State of the Union address that we will read aloud and analyze.

There is a reason to take the time occasionally to read a speech, an article, or an essay aloud in class together. Usually, that type of reading is assigned as homework for this class, but this year, in this one class, there are six students who are on the school's speech and debate teams, three students who are involved with the school's drama club, and one student whose career ambition is to be a television news reporter. So, we put these talents to good use and give these ten students, plus anyone else in the class, opportunities to develop their public speaking skills.

During the next week, each student will work in a group of three to five students to write a State of the Union address. Each person in the group will present part of his or her group's address to the class standing at a podium that looks as presidential as we can make it. We finished the first State of the Union speech and then we read a second State of the Union speech from another president, of another political party, and another decade of the twentieth century. The students do impressive work to compare and contrast the two addresses. After we identify some requirements of a proper State of the Union address, and after we list some current political issues, at least three of which must be included in each group's original State of the Union address, the students separated into their previously chosen groups and worked together for twenty minutes. I move from group to group. The insights, ideas, analysis, and give-and-take of group creativity were fascinating. Presidents should recruit these students to be on the White House professional speech-writing staff.

One student in a group is not participating much. I decide to join that group, and I ask the silent student what he thinks the address should include on the issue of taxes. This student is doing a separate research project on the history of the income tax and on alternatives to the current income tax. "Oh, you mean we can include our topic in this speech, too? Great. I'd suggest that we call for elimination of a lot of tax loopholes. So many people get out of paying their taxes. It's legal, but it's not helping." As he continued his comments, I smiled, I encouraged him to keep doing the great thinking, and then I kept checking on each group.

Group work has advantages and disadvantages. I know of some teachers who assign students to work in groups and then the teacher grades papers or does something on the computer. That's not teaching. When my students are assigned group work, each person is required to be involved and that includes me. It's an opportunity for me to have direct, face-to-face interaction with each student as I move from group to group, listen to each student, ask questions of students, and learn with the students.

The first block class was given thirty minutes to work together instead of the twenty minutes I had planned originally because they were so productive. Continuing their high-quality work was the best use of our time.

With about ten minutes to go in class, the groups completed their work for today. The Internet was working again, so we watched the news report, which was about a Supreme Court decision dealing with a law that regulates political campaign contributions and finances. The role of money in politics was a topic we were researching in anticipation of a debate in class about whether public financing of presidential campaigns and congressional campaigns would be constitutional and beneficial.

At 10:00, the bell rang to end first block class. We had completed everything on our plan for class today. In the final minute of class, we confirmed our plans for the next two weeks. As the students left class, and as the hallways quickly filled with the sounds, energy, and urgency of high school students in motion, I stood by the entry of my classroom door to help monitor the hallway traffic and to talk with ninth graders as they came to our second block civics class.

The schedule this year means that I have two classes of ninth-grade civics and four classes of twelfth-grade political science. On our block schedule A days, I have three classes of political science. On block schedule B day, I have one class of political science to begin the day and then two classes of civics. Each teacher has one planning period out of the four blocks of time each day. On A day, I plan during second block, and on B day, I plan during fourth block. Another teacher floats into my classroom during my planning periods because the school is so crowded. I usually work in the library, a computer lab, or my classroom during plan period, but the working conditions in any of those places are not ideal. I wonder sometimes if people who work in other places have to deal with getting moved around during their day.

At 10:05, the bell rings, and I am standing at the door to close it. Anyone who arrives after that bell rings and the door closes is marked as tardy. As students accumulate tardies, the school imposes penalties. My students are rarely tardy for class at any time of the day. It's due to the e-mail I send to their parents or guardian and the actions those families take. One parent came to school once and stayed all day with her daughter to see where the classes were, what the hallway crowding was like, and how she was doing in her classes. The mother said to her daughter, "I'm thirty-one years older than you are. I can get from your class to the next class in two or three minutes. You get five minutes. Quit talking so much, and you'll be on time. That's that." The student was never tardy to my class or to any other class I know of.

Teaching ninth graders is a completely different endeavor than teaching high school seniors. I like both. My preference is seniors because they bring more life experiences, they bring their knowledge from three more years of high school classes, they are making vital decisions about what they will do after they graduate from high school, and they have some once-in-a-lifetime moments that occur for people only during the senior year of high school.

It is my preference to teach seniors, but the ninth graders, I like to think, need me. Sure, other people teach ninth-grade civics classes at this school. I cannot teach all of the ninth graders or all of the seniors at this school, but I make the contributions that one determined teacher can make.

I cannot control the master schedule, although I do tell the assistant principal who designs that schedule what my preferences are. When I get exactly what I asked for, it is encouraging. When other decisions are made and I get, for example, four civics classes and two political science classes, I make it work.

At 10:05, my second block B-day ninth-grade civics class is ready to start. In the five minutes that pass between the seniors leaving and the ninth graders arriving, three years also pass. I have to mentally shift gears. At this moment, I am teaching fourteen-year-olds, some of whom are still bewildered by a high school that is three or four times larger than their middle school. A few minutes earlier, I was teaching seventeen- and eighteen-year-olds who drive cars, have part-time jobs, pay taxes, are or soon will be registered to vote, and are excited about the college application process or about other options they are pursuing for life after high school.

Some ninth graders adjust quickly and easily to the size, freedom, classes, opportunities, and responsibilities of high school. Other ninth graders are so accustomed to the multiple support systems they had in middle school that ninth grade is a serious struggle. Some educators recommend a separate school just for ninth graders. Other people prefer the old junior high school arrangement, which could include grades 6 through 9 or 7 through 9 and the high school would include grades 10 through 12. Other people make those decisions. I decided years ago to make the most of what I face every day and of whom I face every day.

Teaching ninth graders requires structure, variety, more structure, more variety, rewards, penalties, and a willingness to adjust what you had planned to do when you realize that something is working better than you expected or when you realize that something else is not working at all.

Today, class began perfectly. I asked students to think of a rule at school that they thought was unfair. We were going to evaluate how rules at school are thought of, implemented, evaluated, and changed. We would then compare and contrast that process of how rules are made with how a bill becomes a law in the national government. We were about five minutes into a great discussion when there was a PA announcement about students who had signed to see a college representative needing to know that the 10:15 meeting with the representative had to be rescheduled for 2:00 this afternoon. A few moments after that announcement ended, the telephone in the classroom rang, and that took me away from teaching long enough to tell the assistant principal that, yes, I would send the student he needed to see in the office. About one minute after that, there was a knock on the door. A student office aide was coming to get a student from class whom a school counselor needed to see. By the time all of that had happened, we had lost the momentum of our earlier discussion.

Do I try to get us back to that topic or not? Of course I try, but maybe I could somehow benefit from all of these interruptions. I asked the students, "What would you think of this being a new rule at school: there can be no PA announcements made during class." The conversation that followed had all the unique thinking that can come only from ninth graders.

"It would violate the freedom of speech. If the principal has to talk to us on the PA system, he has the freedom to speak to us."

"It would violate freedom of the press. The PA is like a radio or television. We get news over the PA system."

"I think it violates our right to privacy. The PA invades our classroom."

"The rule just says no PA during classes. The PA can be used before classes or between classes or right after school. It's not violating any rights. It's just, you know, it's just making time for all rights."

"Do we really think this would ever become a rule? The principal and other people in the office make those PA announcements. Don't they run the school? Why would they take the PA away from themselves?"

Amazing. I would greatly prefer to have no knocks on the door during class, no phone calls during class, and no PA announcements during class. I hope those changes can happen someday. Maybe I'll put those on my someday list. But at least the ninth graders and I were able to get back on our subject for the day. I could not control the interruptions, but I could manage the class by creatively applying those interruptions to the topic the students and I were scheduled to learn about today.

Our discussion led us to a list of questions about how rules are made at our school. The students were instantly committed to becoming experts on the process of rule making at their high school. My goal was for them to master the process of how a bill becomes a law, so I could not let the rules at school dominate our time and effort. I had to manage our work on rules so that topic could lead to a deeper understanding of laws.

Making the connection between rules the students experience at school daily and the process of a bill becoming a law meant I needed to manage effectively. So I asked the direct questions: What is similar about the school rule process and U.S. law-making process? What is different about those processes? I challenged the students to identify ten similarities and ten differences. They found thirteen of each. Then we analyzed our lists; the learning was unlimited.

That quality and quantity of learning is always my dream as a teacher. There are times when the dream comes true. Some of those times are the result of perfectly planning the ideal lesson and implementing that lesson in ways that would impress Socrates. Other times, there is an unexpected opportunity as a student offers a comment that can become a learning resource for everyone or as classroom interruptions become a reason to analyze how rules are made at school as a case study in the political process of decision making for public policy purposes.

There was one student who caused a minor problem during second block class. He thought I did not see him doing his math homework. One of the major rules in my classroom is to devote 100 percent attention to our work right here, right now. I tell the students that I do not come to their other classes, their sports practices, or the cafeteria at lunch and interrupt what they are doing so we can work on civics or political science. They are required to not bring work from other classes or social discussion about various activities to this class when we are doing our work.

The process is as follows: the student gives me the work that was being done for another class, and they can come to my room after school to do civics or political science work to make up for the time they wasted in our class. After they complete that after-school work, I give them the other work they were doing. I e-mail their parent or guardian. I tell the student and the family that a second violation means the family has to come to school to meet with me and I would give the work the student was doing for another class to the parent or guardian. The second offense also results in a discipline referral for defiance.

The average is two second offenses each semester, which means 98 or 99 percent of the students avoid second offenses. For that matter, about 95 percent avoid first offenses. Percentages like that equal an A grade, so my dream would be 100 percent obedience, but if I can get A-level obedience, that is an admirable result.

Second block class ended with the bell at 11:35. With one minute left in class at 11:34, the class members had been reminded of their reading assignments for the next week. I took half a minute and had each student answer this question: when is our next test? Each student, one at a time, said, "Monday." Those thirty seconds of direct interaction with each student provided confirmation that everyone knows when the next test is. I find that is more effective than loudly stating as the bell rings and the students leave class, "Remember, our test is next Monday."

As one group of ninth graders exits my classroom and another group of ninth graders enters, I stand by the door to help the administrators supervise the hallways. Teachers are asked to do this whenever possible. There are times when a student from your last class needs to ask a question, and that is done best in the classroom, or a teacher may need to return a phone call quickly during the time between classes, but most teachers get out in the halls when possible. Of course, you have to keep an eye on your classroom also, so what teachers can do to help in the halls is limited by the reality that it does no good to prevent a hallway problem while our brief absence from the classroom gave some students the chance they needed to see what they could get away with.

This class, third block civics, begins at 11:40 and ends at 1:40. Those two hours will include thirty minutes for lunch. This class has lunch from 12:10 to 12:40, so we have part of class, then lunch, and then the rest of class. There is no other way to feed this entire student body than to stagger four thirty-minute lunch periods throughout the two hours of third block class. It is not the ideal schedule for learning, but it is reality.

To make the most of this schedule, I create a thirty-minute activity for the class that begins and ends before lunch. I create a logically connected but separate activity or series of activities for the hour we have after lunch. I have learned through the years that ninth graders accomplish more with these finite portions of work, especially if class is divided by lunch. It is different with seniors. They can be halfway through a sentence when the bell sounds for lunch, go to lunch, return, and finish the incomplete sentence with perfect continuity. The ninth graders will be able to do that in three years.

The topic is rules, but because lunch is coming up, we put that anticipation to good use. The bigger topic is how a bill becomes a law, but rules at school will serve as our introduction as in the earlier class. With lunch only thirty minutes away, I give each student a copy of each of the following: the rules for proper conduct in our school cafeteria; nutrition data for the food items that will be served today in the school cafeteria; and some guidelines from the federal government that public school cafeterias participating in the federal government school lunch program must follow. I explain what the students are receiving, and I tell them to take five minutes for silent indoor reading. They think that is a clever way of reminding them that reading time means no talking, no movement, and no requests to go anywhere.

The nutrition data got the most response from the students. They applied their knowledge from the ninth-grade biology class and from their middle school health classes in ways that showed sophisticated reasoning. They also got in a two-minute debate about ingredients of school pizza versus restaurant pizza. To make the most of that, I asked if they knew what rules restaurants have to follow. "They get inspected. I saw one with an inspection score of 92. That is so bad." "Yeah, my brother works at a restaurant. He says they keep the place really clean. What he can't believe is what people get paid. It's not much. Aren't there any rules about that?"

We agreed that one student would ask the cafeteria manager about rules that restaurants follow. One student mentioned that his mother had a friend who owned a restaurant. Maybe the restaurant owner could visit our class. When everyone left for lunch, that student and I e-mailed his mother to ask about the guest speaker possibility. She replied before the students were back from lunch that the restaurant owner would be glad to visit. We scheduled it for two days from now during the first half hour of class. My hope is that the students will learn more about how laws impact businesses and how businesses work to influence what is put in laws, and I hope that some of the students will set themselves up for a job interview in a year or two by impressing the restaurant owner so much with their manners and intellect that she will hire them when they start looking for a part-time job. I e-mailed the principal about our guest speaker.

The hour of class following lunch is usually divided into three or four different activities. There are academic links between the activities, and sometimes two activities are enough, but one continuous activity for ninth graders to do for one hour right after lunch is not realistic.

Today, my lesson plan calls for a short video showing commercials about food products and the type of information or disclaimers advertising rules require, followed by analysis of some food packages to see what information must be provided to consumers; then we will read part of the school's Student Conduct, Rights, and Responsibilities booklet, and finally, we'll consider changes in the content and format of that student booklet. The overall goal is to increasingly understand the use of rules everywhere in our society. We will also place emphasis today and in the next two class sessions on how rules, regulations, and laws are created.

As we approach 1:39, the results are good. The commercials and the food packages were instantly recognized by the students. The student booklet got some groans, but we turned those initial complaints into a real reason to better understand that booklet. No student had read it entirely, but several students had complaints about what they assumed was in the conduct, rights, and responsibilities booklets. What a perfect opportunity that was to discuss the importance of knowing the law or the rule. There were enough copies of the booklet for every student to keep one. I told them to read the entire booklet before our next class. With that reading background, we could better begin our next class with the completion of students' ideas for improvements in the content and format of the student conduct, rights, and responsibilities booklet.

With about a half minute left in class, I asked, "When is our next test?" Each student, one at a time, answered, "Monday." About two seconds after the final "Monday" answer was heard, the 1:40 bell rang to end class time for instruction. When I see a student start to pack up with several minutes remaining in class, I'll ask, "Does the football team walk off the field when they still have a few minutes left on the clock?" If any student replies, "No, but this is not football," they hear me explain, "You are exactly right. This is your education, so it is actually more important than football. Let's get back to work." That exchange is needed only once or twice per year in any class to make the point convincing.

Yes, I e-mail the family of any student who packs up early. "I thought you would want to know that Kristen almost cost herself some important education time today. She started packing to leave class while instruction was continuing and we had four minutes left in class. I know she plays soccer, so I asked her if she walks off the soccer field when four minutes remain on the clock. She understood, unpacked, and answered the next question."

At 1:40, the ninth graders leave our class, and I help supervise the hallway area by my doorway. The eleventh-grade U.S. history class students whose teacher uses my classroom during fourth block class today are arriving. That teacher has a long journey from the opposite end of a long hallway to get here. Floating from classroom to classroom is tiring, inefficient, and counterproductive. Administrators or central office people who make these master schedules and chart the hour-to-hour use of the building should come teach for a week and float from room to room. Their charts might be replaced with human reality. It's a dream to think that many of those people would ever do a teacher's job for one week. They intentionally do not teach.

At 1:45, my planning period starts. My to-do list may be longer than my plan period time is, but here's everything I need to do:

1. Make copies of research project assignment for political science.
2. Type civics test, proofread, correct, and make copies.
3. Update calendar on my Web page so students have information about our assignments and tests for the next two to three weeks.
4. Talk to two school counselors about two different students who are of concern to me. One is either making A grades or F grades. Those erratic results could be a warning. The other student has cheated twice in class by copying homework and copying answers on a test. She was caught both times, and the evidence was conclusive, but she insists she did nothing "really wrong" as she put it. Her excuse was "everyone cheats."

5. Register online for a professional development program that will deal with "The C Student." We don't have any programs I know of to help push that C average student out of the ordinary grade into good or great.

6. Write another college letter of recommendation for a student who stopped by the classroom during lunch. He brought his resume, his high school transcript, and a newspaper story about a community service project he helped organize. I taught him when he was in ninth grade, and his achievements have been inspiring to watch over these high school years.

7. Fill out a form from an assistant principal about how we use technology to improve instruction.

8. Finish that online electronic recommendation I began about 8:20 this morning from the retired teacher who would like to do some substitute teaching.

I will not get everything on my to-do list completed during this planning period. It will take all of planning period plus an hour or two hours after school to finish all of this. After school, I have to attend a committee meeting about ninth-grade success. We continue to search for ways to help more ninth graders make a successful transition from middle school to high school.

I have to leave school by 5:15 to pick up David and Andrea at their high school after their soccer and marching band practices. Our family puts a high priority on being together each day at breakfast and each night at supper. It is my turn to cook tonight, so that limits the menu to the few items I know how to cook. Fortunately, everyone likes my version of an indoor picnic, so we'll stop at a local grocery store that has a great deli and buy the supplies. After that, David and Andrea will have homework to do. Lauren's hobby is to quilt. Her grandmother taught her how, and she loves making quilts. She does high-technology work all day and then nineteenth-century quilting in the evening. I'll read a book I plan for my political science class to use in a few weeks.

That's it. A day in the life of this high school teacher. Was it what you expected? The day was generally what I expected, but there were some surprises, interruptions, and opportunities that happened. It was a good day. I'll be eager to teach again tomorrow. The realities of teaching are never easy, but the dream of teaching my students as well as my best teachers taught me is one of the reasons I persist.

The reader is asked to reflect on this day in the life of Mr. Joseph Chrisman, high school teacher. What aspects of, events in, and situations during this day could Joe not control or not manage?

Now, think deeply about every aspect, event, situation, decision, and moment during this day when Joe could control or could manage what happened. Make a list of those times when Joe could control or could manage what happened:

1.

2.

3.

4.

5.

6.

7.

8.

9.

10.

11.

12.

13.

14.

15.

16.

17.

18.

19.

20.

Some of the events of the day are beyond what Joe can control or manage. He can control and manage how he responds to those events.

The list above shows twenty events, decisions, and opportunities that Joe could control or manage. Is that more control by the teacher or less control by the teacher than you expected? Is that more opportunity to manage what you do as a teacher or fewer opportunities to manage what you do as a teacher than you expected?

What do these relative amounts of cannot control versus can control and cannot manage versus can manage tell you about the reality of teaching? What do they tell you about the dream of teaching? What do they reveal about your aptitude for and comfort level with being a teacher? If you are already a teacher, what do they tell you about how you could strengthen the control of and the management of the work you do as a teacher?

Did you notice how very little interaction Mr. Chrisman had with other adults at school? Teachers spend their workdays with students who are generally in the five-year-old to eighteen-year-old range. For people who work best with adults, being a classroom teacher is not the best fit. For people whose talents and goals relate to working with children and teenagers on their education, the classroom is the place where that work is done so the classroom is the place where you must be.

Kim Raymond had an idea that she hoped could benefit students and teachers at Jefferson Middle School. The idea cost zero dollars, no money at all. The idea involved no new laws and no new taxes. The idea was to tell more parents and guardians when their child did something good at school.

Kim intended this to be a way for teachers to notice much more intentionally that each day at school included many good results, good achievements, and good interactions. Most students did what they were supposed to do at school. In fact, Kim checked the discipline reports from the prior school year and realized that 84 percent of the students had no discipline incident or action recorded at all. A further analysis showed that 77 percent of the discipline referrals were dealing with misbehaviors committed by 8 percent of the students.

It was easy and perhaps human nature to notice the misbehaviors and not notice the proper behaviors. The misconduct has to be punished and corrected. What is done for students who consistently behave correctly? They are not punished. The absence of punishment, Kim realized, is not a sufficient acknowledgment of people who are doing what is right.

Kim led by example on this. She began sending handwritten WOW notes. The letters in the acronym WOW stand for Wonderful Outstanding Work. The notes were not sent for the ordinary events of a typical day. Just showing up at school did not merit a WOW note. Providing extra, unpaid tutoring sessions before the first class of the day earned a teacher a WOW note.

Eighth graders who helped tutor sixth graders in one teacher's growing early morning tutorial program earned a WOW note and the parent or guardian of those volunteer tutors were called to hear good news about their child.

Kim asked the faculty members to notice the good work that students did and to take two actions. First, in writing, perhaps a comment on a test paper when the student did great writing on an essay question, tell the student how impressive his or her work was. Second, call if possible, or e-mail if the person cannot be reached by phone, to tell the parent or guardian of the student about the good news or the great news.

Kim also encouraged the teachers to share good news reports when they met as grade-level groups or subject matter department groups. Kim's hope was that, as more teachers heard about the good work many students were doing, it would be inspiring. She also hoped that it could help some teachers become aware of ability that students were showing in other teachers' classes that could be applied in all classes.

The WOW notes were effective. Occasionally, a teacher would complain in a faculty workroom conversation that her work was never appreciated. Another teacher complained that the principal should spend her time on "more important stuff than telling her faculty friends how good they are." Some people complain chronically. Kim would not let their complaints prevent her from doing work that was good for the school.

There were many more smiles than there were complaints. Staff members and teachers who received WOW notes genuinely appreciated the vote of confidence. Kim cannot raise the salary of any staff member or teacher, but she can raise the appreciation that is expressed for good work done by staff members and employees.

The student response to the faculty members paying more attention to the good work done by students was most obvious when students started reciprocating. Students knew when a teacher or staff member did something extra for them. The custodian who fixed a student's bicycle was an example. The student told a teacher, and the teacher told Kim, who sent a WOW note to the custodian and then e-mailed the school district's maintenance department supervisor. That custodian was named maintenance department employee of the month. The custodian was given a set of tools that were donated by a local hardware store. That process for that one custodian was an example of the impact the WOW and good news efforts could make.

Kim knew there would always be some students who broke rules, who disobeyed instructions, and, much worse, who violated laws. Kim also knew that most students obeyed rules, followed instructions, and obeyed laws. Kim and the teachers could not perfectly prevent all misbehaviors. But Kim and the teachers could control how they responded to proper behavior. Rather than putting all of the school conduct management system's time and effort toward punishing and correcting misbehavior, Kim was determined to invest equal time and effort toward acknowledging and rewarding good or great behavior.

The reality at Kim's school is that most students behave and that each day some students do superior academic work. The dream is for more and more students to behave and to do superior academic work. Kim's approach is based on the truth that we get more of what we reward.

Kim hoped to do some brain surgery at her school. She liked being the principal, but she had realized that the best position in education is that of teacher. Why? Because teachers spend their time at school in the face-to-face, brain-to-brain, person-to-person adventure of causing learning. Kim was determined to help all teachers have increasingly meaningful career experiences by having increasingly more productive classroom activities, interactions, and results.

Kim had been cautioned that often the principal of a school spends most of the day reacting to problems or incidents. Kim knew she could not prevent all of those situations, but she could control how she responded to them. She was determined to convince the teachers to think of their work in a similar way, yet with one advantage. The teacher does plan what will happen in his or her classroom more than a principal can plan what will happen in his or her workday.

Yes, problems happen in classrooms, but how a teacher responds to those problems and resolves those problems is within the power of the teacher to control and manage.

Yes, great and good results happen in classrooms. How a teacher responds to, acknowledges, appreciates, and is encouraged by those moments is within the power of the teacher to control and manage. The reality of problems need not be allowed to define a day of teaching where the day also included moments when the magnificent dream of teaching was or could be experienced, realized, and treasured.

Laws can be changed. That process can take years of relentless effort. The result, usually a compromise, is a new law that will eventually be challenged, criticized, supported, and changed. There are thousands of laws about education. These laws directly impact what is done and what is not done in public schools.

Teachers can have some impact on making or changing laws about education. Teachers who officially or unofficially organize into groups could increase their impact on laws. Other groups in the political process will be seen and heard. Each teacher will have to decide to what extent he or she becomes involved in the political aspect of the education arena, but know that politics consumes many hours, days, weeks, months, and years of effort that might or might not get the desired results.

School district policies can be changed. That process is political but may not be as complicated or as slow as the state or national political process.

Different perspectives will be considered. Rank in the school district organ-ization chart can be a factor. Which person or which group is most vocal, active, and persistent are factors also. Know that the policymaking or policy-changing process is time consuming and offers no assurance that you will get any part of what you seek. Similar to the process of making laws or changing laws, the policy-making or policy-changing process could result with you getting nothing that you sought.

Theoretically, teachers can impact laws and policies; however, realistical-ly, the return on the investment of time can be questionable. Do the math of time required versus likely results and decide.

In the classroom, working directly with students, there is much that a teacher can control and much that a teacher can manage. Can you think of any factor that is more significant in impacting what happens in a classroom than the teacher? The possibilities for what a capable, conscientious, dedicat-ed teacher can achieve in the classroom with students are unlimited.

The long list of what a teacher cannot control and cannot manage is part of the reality of teaching. The powerful list of what a teacher can control and can manage is also part of the reality of teaching. Which of those two parts of the reality of teaching will dominate? That is largely up to each teacher. Control what you can control. Manage what you can manage.

The list of what a teacher can control and can manage is a vital resource in pursuit of and in attaining the dream of teaching. The dream and the reality of teaching encounter each other daily. Great teachers and good teachers gain inspiration from the dream to master the reality. Other teachers blame the reality for the decline of and loss of the dream. A teacher can control and manage which groups he or she is in.

We turn now to a fundamental, essential, vital question: how do I know if I should be a teacher?

Chapter Seven

How Do I Know If I Should Be a Teacher?

The answer is not "Oh, you'll just know." The answer is not "Well, it will just seem right to you." The answer is not "Eventually, you'll feel this is the job for you and then you'll know to become a teacher." The answer is more precise, more objective, and more certain. The answer is not necessarily 100 percent quantifiable, but the answer is and must be more definite than "You know, it will just, well, it will just fall in place for you."

Consider the following five responses from college students who grew up in a home where one parent was a teacher or where both parents were teachers.

> My parents are teachers. Mom teaches elementary school, and Dad teaches middle school. I guess they like their job; they keep going back every year, but you know, they complain a lot. They seem to find more to complain about than to like. I asked them about that, and they said that, with twenty years of teaching behind them, they were only ten years away from being eligible to retire. I love my parents, but I can't say they love their jobs as teachers. I don't plan to do some job for twenty years and then stay just because I can retire in ten years. I plan to do some job that I really care about and want to do. My parents have shown me that I should not be a teacher. The funny thing is I'm really good with children, but if working with children means the type of career my parents have had, I'll do something else.

> My parents are teachers. Mom teaches high school, and Dad teaches middle school. They love their job. After twenty-two years of teaching, they seem to really look forward to each day at school. I don't get it; I'm glad they like their job, and it's really nice to have them as my personal teachers when I need help with homework or other school stuff. I've seen how some students treat teachers at my school. I would never, I mean never, put myself in that position. I want to love my job as much as my parents love their jobs, but I'm just not cut out to be a teacher.

My mother teaches middle school. My father owns and manages a car repair shop. They both say they do their jobs to make a living. That means they spend ten hours or more every day doing their work just to get paid. I have different ideas for my job. I want to do something that really matters to me and that really has lots of potential to make money. My mother can't do anything about her salary. Dad says his company is profitable, but any slump in the economy means his business suffers. I'm studying business, and I hope to be at the top level of a major corporation someday.

My father taught high school and then became a middle school assistant principal. Now he is a high school principal. He says that each of those jobs has been great. He really likes working at school. His excitement for his job is unlike anything I've seen. My mother works in human resources for a big company. She likes the people and the place, but she is never as excited about her job as my father is about his. I want a career that means as much to me as my father's career means to him. I've had a lot of part-time jobs, but my favorite work is teaching the middle school Sunday school class at our church. Those students and I get along great. I think it would be really good to teach that age group, and that's my plan.

My mother has taught elementary school forever. She has taught the children of students she taught years ago. My mother's students love her. She used to take me to some events at her school, and everyone was so friendly to me. They said I look just like my mother. They wondered if I planned to be a teacher like my mother. I was too young then to really know, but my mother and her mother had chosen teaching as a career. I knew it would be a possibility for me. That was until I did my student teaching. I hated it. How could my mother and my grandmother do this work for decades? I barely got through four months. I am glad for it. Student teaching showed me what I do not want to do. My uncle and aunt have a business they own. I'll work for them and then see what looks best. I sure know what I am not going to do.

Being related to a teacher does not determine the path or fate of your career. Being related to no teachers will not determine the path or fate of your career. Those growing-up experiences can be a factor in a career choice as a child or teenager becomes intrigued with the work a relative does or becomes certain that the relative's work is not of interest. There are many possible factors, reasons, experiences, motives, and inspiration that can impact the answer any particular person gives to the question "How do I know if I should be a teacher?"

As you read this chapter, frequently ask yourself, "How do I know if I should be a teacher?" If you are already a teacher, think through your career experience thus far to see if it is going as planned, better than expected, or not as well as hoped. Depending on what that career experience conclusion is for you, think of ways to move the current reality of your teaching closer to the dream of teaching.

Save the world. That's what I'm going to do. I'll be the teacher who works through schools to save the world.

Is that a dream that could be fulfilled with the proper work and with adequate resources? Is that a fantasy because, among the many reasons, no one teacher is in a position to impact the entire world?

Would an interview for a teaching job include the principal of the school asking the prospective teacher, "Do you intend to save the world if you are selected to teach at our school?" No.

Nothing else worked out, so I'll fall back on my teaching degree. I can get a teaching job and do the least required to stay employed. I'll use my sick days and personal days to look for a better job. I'll just use the textbook and the stuff that comes with it. This should be easy money. I might coach, too. That's more easy money, and I could work on coaching stuff while my students do the work I give them.

Would an interview for a teaching job include the principal of the school asking the prospective teacher, "Do you intend to just pass the time in class by giving the students superficial busy work to do while you work on coaching?" No.

Between the extreme fantasy of "teacher as world saver" and the mundane approach of "teacher as classroom clerk" are some much more reasonable yet honorable motivations to be a teacher. Please add to the following list of motivations to be a teacher and reasons to consider a teaching career.

1. I like working with children.
2. I relate well with teenagers.
3. I had a great teacher who made a big difference in my life, and I want to do that for my students.
4. It seems to have a lot of job security.
5. My grandmothers were both teachers. I got the idea from them and never really considered anything else.
6. Math has always fascinated me. I want to help those students who think they can't do math.
7. I helped coach a baseball team for eight- and nine-year-olds when my little brother was on the team. We got along great. That got me interested in teaching elementary school.
8. My high school football team lost the state championship game by three points my senior year. I was a starter on that team. Since then, my goal has been to be the head coach of a high school football team that wins a state championship. That means I also have to work as a teacher.
9. It's really personal. It's based on what I believe. I think I was born to teach. I really take my faith seriously. I've thought for years that God wants me to be a teacher. I volunteered at a church camp for middle

school students every year during high school and college. It just convinced me I need to work with that age group.

10. When I have been in the classroom of my best teachers, the thought has come to my mind often that I would love to be able to teach as well as they do. No other people in any other job have inspired that thought in me.

11. I don't think I would be good at anything else.

12. I really want to make a difference. I want a job that matters. You always hear that teaching is the most important job. Well, that's what I intend to do because it matters to me that I do something that matters to society.

13. I've had several terrible teachers. I'd like to come back to my old school and show them how it's done.

14. Actually, the money part of teaching appeals to me. Other jobs pay more money, but teaching is steady work with good benefits like health insurance. I've worked at a restaurant during high school and college. I can keep working on weekends and in the summer for extra money. If teaching does not work out, the restaurant owner has told me I can work there full time.

15. The reason for me is students. That's the only reason. I care about students. I get along with students. They learn from me. It's been like that since I was twelve years old and started babysitting. I've just always been good at teaching children whatever they needed to learn.

16. I like school. Of all the places I could work, give me a school. Schools are creative and energetic places. I just can't see myself working behind a desk in some office cubicle forever doing whatever company employees do.

17. I know what a great teacher can do for a student. When my parents got divorced, it was awful. My seventh-grade English teacher was the one person who reached out to me then. She went on to become a high school counselor. I want to be just like her. I want to teach and then be a school counselor.

18. This might not be the best reason, but it's not the worst. I've been a camper and then a counselor-in-training at this great camp in New Hampshire every summer since I was ten. I want to work there every summer. The only job that fits into the camp schedule is teaching. I like the camp, and I work well with the campers. I think school can be like that.

19. I've heard a lot of politicians talk about how they are going to fix education. It's all talk. I'm going to fix education. Some people dream of curing a disease or of inventing some amazing product. I'm going to cure what's wrong in schools. I actually thought about becoming a missionary, but then I realized there's no need to travel to another county to find people or places needing help. Schools right here need help, my help.

20. I love to learn. I want to inspire my students so they will love to learn. Teachers get to spend their lives learning. That's the job I want.
21. Well, it really doesn't look like it is that difficult. Everyone goes to school, so everyone knows what teachers do. I'm not the hardest working person in the world. I had teachers who never seemed to work that much, but you know, they were okay teachers. That looks good to me. Some of them had second or third jobs or owned a small business. I like that plan.
22. I love music. Music is my life. I intend to show students why they should love music. How many other steady jobs are there for musicians?
23. For me, it's all about sports. I was not a great student. I made average grades. I was good at most sports. The only thing that kept me going to school was sports. I should have made better grades, so I'll be a coach, and I'll be sure the athletes on my teams make better grades than I did.
24. I always liked to read. Books fascinate me. It concerns me that more students hate reading. I saw that with my friends in high school. Most of them never took reading assignments seriously. Teaching will put me in a position to show students why reading is so important.
25. You hear about more businesses closing than about schools closing, so the job looks steady. Then there's a program in my state that pays off 25 percent of my college loans for each year I teach in some poverty-area school. Four years of teaching means no debt, some work experience, a good start on a career, and still being young enough to start a different career.
26.
27.
28.
29.
30.

Which of the reasons to become a teacher most directly and most personally apply to you?

Do some of the reasons to become a teacher establish a foundation for a better teacher and a better teaching career?

Does the reason to be a teacher matter once a person begins his or her work in a teaching job? At what point, regardless of the reason to teach or the inspiration to teach, does the job require certain duties to be fulfilled by every teacher?

To apply the concepts within the list of reasons to be a teacher, some profiles will be presented. For each of the people who are profiled, use the description given and your insight to evaluate whether the person should be a teacher or not.

PROFILE 1: SHOULD BRENDA BE A TEACHER?

Hi. I'm Brenda. I'm eighteen years old, and in three months, I'll graduate from high school. These next three months will be the best part of high school. I play softball, and during spring vacation in April, our team is going to a huge tournament in Florida. I'm so excited about that trip. I've got friends on the team, and we've played softball together forever.

By the end of April, I'll decide which college to attend. I think I know now, but I have more time to figure it out. In college, I want to study psychology and business and lots of stuff about sports marketing.

There are a lot of jobs that interest me. My mother is a school psychologist, and that looks interesting. My softball coach is a great coach and a great teacher. She taught my chemistry class last year. It was so hard, but she made it a lot of fun. She says I would be a great teacher and a great coach.

My father works for a radio station. He manages the place. They broadcast a lot of college sports and high school sports. He says that everything related to sports is big business. I think that would be a neat job.

My grades are good. I have a 3.5 average so far, but if this semester is straight As, I could bring my high school average up to 3.6, and I'm really trying to do that. There are some college scholarships that require a 3.5, so I'm good for those, but I'd like to be better. There are more scholarships to apply for even this summer after I graduate from high school and then when I'm in college.

I do some volunteer work at a local hospital. I just run errands for people around this huge hospital building. I get to see everything. Some of those jobs look neat, but I just never saw myself going to medical school and all that stuff.

I'm involved with a program at my high school where we go to an elementary school once or twice a month and read with students. It's been fun. The second-grade teacher whose class I visit said the students really like me. I like helping them learn to read, but if I become a teacher, I would work with middle school or high school. I like softball a lot, so high school is probably the best level for me to teach. But who knows what job I'll end up in?

Two of my high school teachers wrote really wonderful college letters for me. I asked another teacher to write a letter for me to help with a scholarship I applied for. He said he sets a limit of ten letters like that each year because they take a lot of time or something. He was already at the limit, so I asked him too late. I never heard anyone say they had a limit on anything like that. If I'm ever a teacher, I hope I don't give my students the answer that teacher gave me.

Well, now you know some stuff about me. Do you think I should be a teacher?

PROFILE 2: SHOULD JARED BE A TEACHER?

My dream is to be a middle school teacher. It's my dream. I think about teaching all the time. At the start of my sophomore year in college, when we filled out a form to indicate our top three preferences for a major, I wrote teaching, teaching, teaching. I know people who wrote stuff like British literature, premed, or history. I wrote what I dream of doing and what I will do.

I'm a junior in college now. My actual major is a combination of U.S. history, mathematics, and teacher education. My college requires us to major in the academic subjects we are going to teach. So, last year, this year, and next year, I take way above average class loads. I'll take everything I can fit in this summer and then pile it on my last year of college. I can't afford a fifth year of college.

Like I said, teaching is my dream. I have two younger sisters and one younger brother. I've taught them everything from how to play soccer to how to get their chores done at home to how to stay out of trouble. When each of them got in middle school, they went through the typical weird things that everyone does when they are thirteen years old. They came to me for advice, and things went better for them.

It's funny. In high school, they did not ask me for advice very much. I wondered why. I asked my sister, Liz, about that. "Jared, you told us everything we needed to know when we were in middle school. All that still works in high school. High school is bigger, but you told us to do our work on time, never get caught up in dumb gossip, know what each teacher requires, and do those requirements whether we like it or not. It got me through middle school, and it's getting me through ninth grade so far.

All my life, anything I've done that was anything like teaching went really well. What Liz told me was important. If I can get middle school students on the right path, they'll do better in middle school and in high school.

I think I was born to teach, but not elementary school. I had the best elementary school teachers, but I'll never know where they found the patience and then the energy to work with children. I have friends who can't wait to be elementary school teachers. They love the young children. I guess everybody is different. It's important to know what you are best at.

I plan to teach U.S. history and math classes to middle school students. I talked to three seniors at our university who are doing their student teaching now at middle schools. One loves it; another says it's all right but is not what she expected; and the other says it is so bad he is going to take a year after college, get a master's degree in computer science, and maybe work for a technology company instead of teach science and technology to middle school students.

I'll be a student teacher in one year. I know I'll love it. When it gets difficult, so what? Every job that matters at all gets difficult. If it is not what I expected, then it's what it is, and I need to know that.

Well, based on what you know about me, should I be a teacher?

PROFILE 3: SHOULD CHAD BE A TEACHER?

I'm Chad. I'm a senior in college. I'm sitting here in a seminar for people who are student teaching this semester and who will graduate from college in May. Most people in this seminar are super stressed about finding a teaching job. I mean, some of these people never think of anything but completing one more employment application from another school district, even if they have already filled out ten, twenty, or more applications.

Me, I'm actually listening to what the professor and the other seniors are saying about their student teaching experiences. It's March of our senior year in college. We graduate in May. We'll be eligible for schools to interview us in May. But I don't feel ready for all of that.

Student teaching has not been what I expected. I was in high school just a few years ago. Could things have changed that much in five years or so? Maybe I look at it differently now. Getting the high school students I am working with to listen is not easy. The teacher I am assigned to, well, he's not the best. He's not the worst, either, but when I was observing his classes in January and part of February, before I started teaching one chemistry class, I was always worried that I would go to sleep. Where did he find all of those videos about chemistry, and why does he show so many of them? Students should do chemistry, not watch a video of other people doing chemistry.

Now I teach two chemistry classes. I took every teacher education class that my college required, but all of those lofty philosophies about learning or knowledge of human growth and development don't mean much with a group of thirty-one high school juniors who are not interested in chemistry. Why did we have to take all of those teacher education classes? Who made that requirement?

I've learned more in the past one month as a student teacher working with my two chemistry classes than I learned about teaching in all of my college teacher certification required classes. My college did help me by requiring a full major in chemistry. Whatever you are going to teach, this college requires you to major in that. So, I have studied chemistry, just like my friends who plan to go to medical school or pharmacy school studied chemistry.

What's helped me the most is that I can explain just about anything dealing with chemistry to my students, well, when they listen.

Maybe I'm just so different from their regular teacher that the students are still adjusting. They probably like all those videos because it was so easy to watch the video or to take a nap. I have not shown one video. Why put chemistry on the movie screen when we can put chemistry right in front of us with experiments?

There's an employment fair on our campus next week. Some of the big pharmaceutical companies will be there. They need sales representatives who understand chemistry. I'm going to talk with them. I hear they pay a lot, train you well, let you earn stock in the company, and pay for graduate school. No school district can pay me a lot, help me invest in stock, or pay for my graduate degree.

The seminar continues with some other seniors saying how difficult student teaching is. They said it was hard to keep up with all the papers to grade. None of those education philosophers whose books we read told us to be ready for tons of papers to grade. Philosophy is interesting, but all of us in this seminar seem to be saying that school is down to earth, but philosophy is up in the clouds. We need to know what works in the real world of schools. It's not philosophy, and it's not videos. I think it is getting students very involved in interesting activities so they participate and learn as they do stuff.

This seminar session is almost over. We meet once each week. Next week, we are supposed to turn in a five-page paper and present our ideas to the class. The topic is "My Philosophy of Education." I think my philosophy of education is, do not have a philosophy. Instead, thoroughly know the subject you are going to teach, and plan activities so the students are involved in learning.

Well, based on my ideas and what you know about me, should I be a teacher?

PROFILE 4: SHOULD JESSICA BE A TEACHER?

I graduate from a big university in one month. I'm twenty-two years old. I have double majored in English and in economics. That is an unusual combination, but my mother is an English teacher in a high school, and my father is a financial planner. I always thought they had interesting jobs, so I got the ideas for my majors from my parents. I also studied Spanish, theater, and psychology as much as possible, along with the usual general requirements.

I applied to some graduate school programs, and I was accepted. I could work on a master's degree in English or business administration, but I've been going to school since I was five years old, and I'm not so sure I want to continue that right now.

One graduate school might possibly work because it can be finished in one demanding calendar year. I would be in graduate school this summer, fall, and then next spring for three straight semesters. I'd finish about a year from now with certification to teach middle school or high school and with advanced work at the graduate level in English or economics. Every middle school has English classes. Every high school has English classes, so that is better for teaching jobs than economics.

Any type of graduate school means more student debt. What job can I get that starts right after I graduate from college? There's a possibility of working for a year in the admissions office of my university. My mother says I could try to get a job in a school as a teacher's aide. That would help me see if I like working at school. She also said I could work at one of those businesses where students are taught by paid tutors.

My mother says I would be a great English teacher. I have made straight As in my college English classes. I worked in the university's library during my junior and senior years in the writing lab. That was a great job. It was a program the librarians and English professors created to encourage college students to appreciate the importance of writing in all academic disciplines. I specialized—not on purpose or by design, but it just worked out this way—in helping economics majors put all of their charts and graphs and statistics into words. Somebody told me I should work for companies that collect a lot of polling data, because I can put the data into words. How does anyone get a job like that?

Well, this university has some alumni who do that type of work, so I could ask them.

My mother really encourages me to work in a school next year to see if I like it. She's convinced I would be such a good high school English teacher. Maybe. I remember that my high school English teachers were good. One of them was the best teacher I ever had. I think he was the other reason I studied English so much in college.

Well, graduation is in thirty-four days. Based on what you know about me, should I be a teacher?

PROFILE 5: SHOULD CATHY BE A TEACHER?

Nine years. I've been doing this for nine years. There was never, absolutely never, any other job that interested me. I always wanted to be an elementary school teacher. As a child, I would pretend to be a teacher. My little friends and I would play school in the basement of my house or outside in a yard or anywhere. I liked it best when I got to play the teacher.

It's strange because I am not related to anyone who is a teacher. There was no person in my family that I know of who was ever a teacher, so I'm not continuing a family tradition. It's just always been my dream to teach elementary school.

I always loved to read. I always loved math. I thought, what could be better than being the person who made sure that everyone in a classroom of children learned to read and learned about arithmetic. I figured that children who mastered those two skills could go on to learn anything.

Nine years. I've been teaching elementary school for nine years. Whatever I expected the job to be is not what the job has become. I thought each year would be new and exciting because of working with a new group of students each year. For some reason, my ninth year of teaching just feels like a repeat of my eighth year of teaching.

Our school has moved to a very structured and rote method of reading instruction. The school bought a new kindergarten through fifth grade reading program, and it is detailed for each day of the year for each grade level. Teachers must follow the daily script and the daily procedures.

We've been doing this for three years. It's taken all of the creativity and all of the humanity out of teaching reading. I read the daily script and the students follow by doing their required tasks. What's worse is that this year we did the same thing for math. The school bought the kindergarten through fifth grade math program from the same company that made the reading program. I would not be surprised if science, social studies, art, and music will be next.

Before long, the school will be a factory with an assembly line of instructional programs and programmed instruction. That is not the job I dreamed of for years. That is not the job I was hired for nine years ago. That is not the job I went to college and graduate school for. It is really difficult to imagine having to do this assembly-line process for the rest of my career.

Other things have changed, too. Students bring so many problems with them to school. Poverty, broken home relationships, medical conditions, learning disabilities, out-of-control misbehavior, psychological syndromes or disorders, difficulties in regular interactions with other children, depression, anxieties, bad habits, and even some drug use by these children. How can I teach reading or math to elementary school students who have difficulties that get worse every year? How can I be their social worker, doctor, therapist, counselor, provider, safety net, and also teacher?

Even if I thought I could do all of this now, it just gets more complicated each year. What's this job going to be like in five, ten, or fifteen years? Can I do this job from now until I retire?

I feel stuck. I wondered about becoming a school counselor or maybe a curriculum specialist. I thought about becoming a principal. I don't know if those jobs would be better or not.

I'm thirty-one years old. I actually thought I would teach for thirty-five or forty years. Is that possible anymore?

I could start in another career. That would break my heart because teaching was always my dream, my heart's desire, and the promise I would keep to myself. That dream seems so far away now. I'm up against nine years of reality, and the dream is barely keeping up. It should not be this way, but I can't deny how different and how difficult this job has become.

I would be glad to work harder, to work more hours, to do most anything. How can I work hard enough to get my students out of poverty? How can I work enough hours to teach a student whose every thought is about her mother who is in prison? How can I touch the lives of my students when every day I have to read some dumb script to them so that we can complete today's reading task, which was designed by people far away who will never know my students?

This is not the job I signed up for nine years ago. Based on what you know about me and about the reality I face, should I continue to be a teacher?

PROFILE 6: SHOULD BRAD BE A TEACHER?

I'm Brad, twenty-eight years old, college graduate, and married for three years; we have a daughter who is four months old. I'm a computer expert. I work in information technology for a consulting firm. I do anything the firm needs or that our clients need. It's interesting work, and it provides the income my family needs.

My wife, Kristen, is twenty-nine years old. She is taking six months off from work to stay at home with our baby. Then Kristen will return to work at the huge regional shopping mall in our community. She is the senior accountant for the property management company that owns the mall building. Her employer has a tenant that is a day care center, so our daughter can go there when Kristen returns to work. It's a clever business idea that offers day care for infants and children while mall shoppers shop or while mall employees work.

Fatherhood is making me think about what I want for our daughter, Lynn. My job takes me out of town often. It concerns me that I'll be out of town on business when Lynn takes her first step or starts talking or who knows what else that I don't want to miss.

It also concerns me that the work I do requires skills that a lot of people don't have. Sure, many people can make computers do anything. What concerns me is work ethic. Whenever my company interviews people who are right out of college, so many of them say they want their job to be fun. Who told them to say that? Who told them to expect that? It's a job. It's work. Fun is at amusement parks or movies.

I can't solve all of society's work ethic problems, but I know how I got my nothing-can-stop-me work ethic. My family set the example, and some of my teachers set the same example. So I've been thinking that it might be good for Lynn if I started doing what it takes to become a high school computer teacher. Imagine the extra time I would have with my family instead of sitting in airports all over the country.

Money is a factor. Teaching would never pay what my information technology job pays, but I would probably move into school administration after a few years. They make a lot more money than teachers. I've been promoted three times with my current employer, so I think I would move up the ranks in a school system.

My college major was computer science. I did not think back then of becoming a teacher, but I've checked with some nearby colleges and some online programs. I could get teaching certification in two years with one program that gives some credit for my work experience with computers.

I don't know much about what it would be like to work in a school. I've always worked with computers and for a company. I just have this idea that high school students need to know what I could teach them. I could prepare them for the reality of the world of work.

Kristen and I have talked about this. She sees good points and bad points. So do I. I don't want to wake up twenty years from now and wish I had been a teacher. I don't want to wake up five years from now and wish I had stayed in information technology instead of gone into teaching. Based on what you know about me, do you think I should be a teacher?

One method used to determine who should be a teacher in general and who should be selected to fill a specific teaching job vacancy is the interviewing process. Interested and qualified candidates complete the applications from school districts, providing the usual information about educational background, work experience, references, and answers to other questions that each school district decides to include.

Some school districts include on their application a multitude of questions designed to probe in detail the skills, motivations, and judgment of the candidate. Some school districts may use the application merely to confirm that candidates have the fundamental teacher certification and any other legal, regulatory, or policy requirements. Those districts would then use the interview process to obtain details about candidates.

School district websites often include the information about the application process and often include the application itself. Increasingly, a candidate completes the application online. Follow-up by the school district could include an initial e-mail to confirm receipt of the electronic application and then a later e-mail or letter to state that all application materials—college transcripts, teacher certification certificate, test scores, letters of recommendation, and other requirements—have been received and the application is now active, so school administrators can consider the candidate for teaching vacancies for which he or she is qualified.

The application process, screening of applications, interview sequence, and final selection of a new hire can be more or less bureaucratic, structured, rigid, and formal depending on factors such as laws, policies, the size of a school district, and the workplace culture or "local ways of doing things." Some schools and some principals may welcome phone calls, e-mails, letters with resumes, and an in-person inquiry at the school. Other schools and other principals may not welcome, may not allow, or may not have the option to consider such direct contact because all personnel matters are managed, at least in the early stages, by the school district officials. Know how the application process works in each school district you apply to, and put as much energy, effort, and persistence into the job search as possible.

When a person interviews for a teaching job, is selected for that teaching job, and is officially hired for that teaching job, there is some confirmation that this person should be a teacher. Some confirmation is not total confirmation, so there are additional questions to be answered.

Does every person who is hired for a teaching job, who accepts the job offer, and who does the job during the time of his or her contract become a teacher who remains in an education career throughout his or her life? Does every person who is hired for a teaching job get hired again for a second year? Which of the people who are hired for a teaching job succeed in the job, excel in the job, just barely avoid getting fired, actually do get fired, or eventually quit on their own?

The interviewing process is designed to identify the best match. A teaching job at a certain school is vacant. The school district has twelve qualified applicants for this position. Which candidate of these twelve is best suited for the teaching position? What is revealed through the interview process? How can the interview process help a person answer the question "Should I be a teacher?" The answer could be yes, but not at this school where I am being interviewed now; yes, but not for the job I am interviewing for now; yes, this is the perfect job in the perfect school for me; yes, but maybe not now; or maybe, but it is going to require a very precise fit between the right job and me.

The answer from any one interview is rarely going to be an absolute no, but an interview or a series of interviews could cause a person to begin thinking that what schools seek and what the prospective teacher expected the job of teaching to be just do not match up well. Use the interview process to learn about a school, a school district, one specific job, and yourself; however, no one interview is the part that defines the totality of you and of your career. Each interview can and should increase your knowledge of teaching and of yourself. With that in mind, let's read the interview transcript from three candidates for a middle school sixth-grade teaching position. The interviewing committee includes the principal, a school counselor, a seventh-grade math teacher, a sixth-grade English teacher, and the mother of an eighth-grade student. As the transcripts are read, think in general whether the people being interviewed should be teachers, and think which of these three candidates, if any, stand out as the superior choice.

Nathan is a recent college graduate. He is looking for his first teaching job. Phillip graduated from college three years ago. He has worked for a city government for two and a half years after college graduation while he went to graduate school part time to begin an alternative path to teacher certification. He completed that certification program in the last five months when he did student teaching. Claire is currently teaching high school math. She has five years of teaching experience. She is interested in moving to a middle school teaching position.

For the benefit of efficient comparisons, the interview question will be given followed by the three separate answers of Nathan, Phillip, and Claire. Please note: the interviews would be conducted separately, not with the three candidates together in a group interview. Please note also: space is provided for the reader to answer each question. As the answers from Nathan, Phillip, and Claire are given, think of what your answers would be. If your area is elementary school or high school, you can make some adjustments, or you can put yourself in the role of a teacher candidate for a job you had not considered but might find interesting.

Then, read through the answers given by Nathan, Phillip, and Claire to see who, if anyone, from those three would be selected for the job. If you were the fourth candidate for this job and you were being evaluated against Nathan, Phillip, and Claire, would you be selected for the job?

First interview question: We like to begin by giving you an opportunity to fully introduce yourself. Then we have five specific questions. But, first, what would you like us to know about you that relates to being a middle school math teacher of sixth graders?

Nathan: I like middle school students, and I like math. I graduated from college one month ago with a major in mathematics and with middle school certification to teach. I also have high school certification, but it's the curiosity and the energy of the middle school students that I really am fascinated with. I have done volunteer work with a college program that partners future teachers with middle school students who need a mentor. I had a wonderful student teaching experience for two months at a middle school where I taught sixth and seventh graders. My student teaching included two months at a high school. I taught geometry and Algebra II. It was good, but I just see a better fit for me in middle school.

Phillip: I graduated from college three years ago. I majored in math. I took every math class there was to take. I've always been good at math. For most of the time since college, I have worked in the local juvenile justice system, and I have gone to graduate school part time. It became so obvious to me that most juveniles who are arrested, found guilty, and incarcerated were failing in school. The juvenile justice experts tell me that they deal with younger offenders than ever. So I decided to do whatever it took to become a teacher. Those middle school students need help. It's my dream to help them. I've used my math skills to analyze a lot of data about juvenile crime. The conclusion I reached is that doing better in school helps reduce the likelihood of a thirteen-year-old breaking laws. That's why I want to teach middle school math.

Claire: I've taught high school math for five years. My students have learned a lot of math. My advanced students can do college-level math. My basic students struggle with fundamental arithmetic. It is obvious that a lot our ninth graders in high school were not ready for high school and sure were not ready for high school math. I've done a lot of work in our school district with middle school and high school math teachers who want to create a smooth transition for students as they go from middle school math to high school math. I think the best way to support that is to work in a middle school myself. I know what the students need to succeed in high school. It's my hope to show the middle school students how to fully prepare for high school success, especially in math.

Reader:

Second interview question: What would you do to accommodate the range of skills and abilities in middle school students, especially sixth graders? Some of them do work above grade level, while others are at grade level, and still others are below. How would you deal with this?

Nathan: I took a very helpful college class on how to teach gifted and talented students. I also took a great class in teaching the unmotivated and underachieving student. My student teaching experience was an amazing reality check. Those college classes were interesting and had some good ideas, but what seemed to matter most in my teaching was getting to know the students. They all have interests or hobbies. If they like cars, I show them how math relates to buying a car. If they like food, we do all kinds of math problems or statistical analysis with food calculations. It seemed to work with all the groups you mentioned. As they saw my interest in them, they got more interested in math.

Phillip: I know the students who are below grade level. The juvenile justice system is filled with them, but there are some—not as many, but some—juvenile offenders who are much smarter than they want their friends to know. They think it's not cool to make good grades. That's part of what schools are up against—a group of students who encourage each other to fail in school. Here's my idea. Start vocational education in fifth grade. Identify the students who are not college material, who are already writing off school, and put them in a fifth-grade introduction to vocational school. Then in middle school, these students are in vocational school all day, but it includes math and English and other basics. It's learning math by building furniture or learning English by reading the instructions for repairing computers.

Now, for the students who are at grade level or above, get creative. I hated middle school when I was a student. We did the same thing in every class, and almost all we took was English, math, science, and social studies. We took them every year. Get creative. Have a class in astronomy. Middle school students like stars and planets and space travel. Have a class in cooking, carpentry, or entrepreneurship. Put the energy of the students to use.

Claire: Every school has that problem. Here's how I deal with it. I tell the students to be very honest with me and explain two things: what in math makes the most sense to you, and what in math makes the least sense to you? That tells me more than any diagnostic quantifiable test can reveal because it is in the language of each student. They are blunt in what they tell me. Then I design instruction to build on what makes sense to them and lead them to figure out what had not made sense before. It works. They begin to realize how much they knew and how much more they can learn. It works for all of the groups you mentioned. It takes a lot of my time, but it gets results, it virtually eliminates remediation, and it is the type of extra effort I promised myself I would always invest in my students.

Reader:

Third interview question: School budgets are tight and will get tighter. How can you make sure your students learn all they should if budgets for books, technology, classroom supplies, and other resources used by teachers and students have to be cut?

Nathan: One of the best math lessons I did with middle school students involved cereal boxes. There are a lot of numbers on those boxes. Middle school students know a lot about breakfast cereals, so each student either brought in a box or used a box I provided. I asked teachers in the school to bring in boxes, so we had plenty. There was no cost to anyone. Then students did all kinds of math calculations based on the nutritional data and other information on their cereal box. As budgets get tighter, we need to get more creative with what we do. We also need to ask people to share or to donate.

Phillip: I've seen the same thing happen in local government. The juvenile justice budget was cut 2 percent last year and another 3 percent this year. Everyone was asked to submit ideas that would cut costs. The first budget cut meant a few job vacancies were not filled when people retired or quit. That increased the workload of everyone else. The second year, all travel was eliminated, so no person could attend any continuing education conference that was out of town. We just created our own training and spent no money on travel or other costs associated with our professional continuing education. I think schools call it professional development. So if teachers work together to trade their best ideas instead of traveling to conferences that cost money to attend, that part of the budget can be cut easily.

Claire: My answer is to seek grant money. It's amazing how many organizations, foundations, professional groups, and other associations like to fund programs in education. Governments sometimes have grant money available. So any school or school district can apply for grants. The more you apply for, the more you could get. It's like what we tell future college students about applying for scholarships during their senior year of high school. My school got a twenty-thousand-dollar grant last year for an innovative math and science teaching method, in which two teachers were trained at no cost. The grant included textbooks, computer programs, and other supplies. So when budgets are cut due to any reason, some of the lost money can come from grants.

Reader:

Fourth interview question: Teaching in middle school is different from any other teaching. This is a unique age group. Tell us your overall philosophy of education as it relates specifically to middle school students, and then tell us how your philosophy of education relates to grades students are given.

Nathan: I've actually thought about that a lot. I took a philosophy of education class in college. It was interesting, but what does anyone actually do with that philosophy stuff when you teach? No student I met in my student teaching or in any other work ever cared about my philosophy of anything. So I wrote a paper saying that my philosophy of education is really a nonphilosophy. I wrote about a middle school student who never cared about school until one teacher just kept showing the student that school was cool. The student likes music, sports, and pizza, so this math teacher creates all these math activities about music, sports, and pizza. It was not perfect. The student still had troubles, but that student made a C on a math test, and when he got the paper back, he said for all to hear, "I never passed a math test before. How did that happen?" The teacher said, "Easy. You did the work. You understood the math. I'm confident you will keep making good grades." So, it's not about philosophy with me. It's about people. As for grades, with some students—maybe most—they get in habits. If you are used to failing, you keep failing. If you are used to As, you keep making As. I look for ways to get the failing students to see themselves differently. Is that a philosophy or a way of getting results?

Phillip: Some people say that middle school is unique. I would be more direct. It's a strange age but a fascinating age. So much happens during those years of twelve, thirteen, and fourteen, and so much can happen that is good or bad. These middle school students seem to be at extremes. They like you one day. They hate you the next day. My philosophy about middle school education is to expect the unexpected. As for grades, the numbers are facts. If a student plays basketball and hits two of ten free throws, he knows that is failure in free throws. Don't tell him he did great when he missed eight out of ten. Same in the classroom. Be straight with the students. They know the facts, and they are not going to benefit from being given a passing grade if they deserved a failing grade.

Claire: To be honest, my philosophy of middle school is about 50 percent middle school and 50 percent from the old junior high school approach. There are good points about both. The middle school really addresses the unique human growth and development issues of this age group but can sometimes make that a higher priority than academics. The junior high approach says that academic preparation for high school is the top priority and the socialization or other parts get less attention. I would balance those instead of picking one approach or the other. My experience with grades is that students just look at the number. Students see a 76, 84, 52, or 100 percent and may not analyze what they did correctly and what they did wrong. When I return papers, we always take time for each student to analyze his of her own grade, not their friends' grades. They like to see if they did better or worse than other people. I need them to see if they did better or worse than their last grade. I also expect them to figure out if they did the best they could have or if they made avoidable errors. I use grades as a way to measure student achievement and as a way for them to learn about their learning.

Reader:

Fifth interview question: The topic of classroom management is important. This includes your classroom discipline system and everything else you do to manage your classroom. What are your thoughts on that?

Nathan: I have been told that great teaching is the best classroom-management system. I believe that great teaching is also the best way to prevent— well, to reduce—misbehaviors. Some students resist the best efforts of any teacher. I do believe that almost all students will cooperate if the teacher provides interesting classroom activities for students so they concentrate on learning instead of other stuff. I will certainly make all of the rules 100 percent clear. I'll teach the rules, and on the second day of school, we will have a test on the rules. Everyone gets a copy of the rules. I'll post the rules in the classroom and on my website. I will structure my classroom procedures to match the fact that middle school students benefit from having a sequence of two or three or so different learning activities during a class. We are asking for students to get in trouble if we tell them to sit down, read a chapter, and write answers to questions, all with total silence for an hour.

Phillip: My juvenile justice system work has put me in the most severe classroom-management system this age group faces. If they are in our custody, they are completely managed every minute of the day. Obviously, schools are different. There is one major lesson I have learned that does apply. Children and teenagers who have unsupervised time on their hands are more likely to cause trouble than if they have much supervision and many responsibilities. So, of course, I would have rules in my classroom. I would have a proper procedure for everything we do. I would constantly, I mean constantly, monitor what every student is doing. I will not give them busy work and then go to my desk to do computer stuff. Police officers set up some crime prevention systems with additional and obvious presence of officers. I'll do that type of aggressive monitoring in my classroom.

Claire: I tend to think optimistically, so I reward the desired behavior. I know some students will break rules or disobey instructions, and I'll deal with them by the book. Students will know the rules, and they will know the price to pay for violating the rules long before they disobeyed. Students will also know that, when they cooperate fully and if they cooperate all the time, I'll reward them. They don't just avoid punishment; they earn recognition. They might get some computer time or an e-mail to their parent. Students have told me that e-mail to their parents about good behavior or good work at school has resulted in extra rewards at home. So, I'll have a highly structured classroom with exact rules and instructions. I'll emphasize the benefits of doing what is supposed to be done.

Reader:

Sixth interview question: How would you keep in touch with parents and guardians? How would you seek to involve them? What would you do if a parent or guardian did not respond to your request to help their child improve?

Nathan: Phone calls, e-mails, and letters mailed home—all of those can help. Lots of information on the school website and on my teacher website would help. I would let parents know they are welcome to visit class. I would let them know my schedule so we can set up meetings before school or after school. For the parents or guardians who do not respond, my assumption is that something is wrong. They have problems at home or at work. Maybe the student is intercepting the letters or e-mails. I would ask a school counselor or a social worker to help reach that parent. I would ask other teachers to see how they reach that parent. Maybe the elementary school the student attended knows who in that family can be reached and how to reach them.

Phillip: I guess I won't be able to use a court order, but I will be able to go the extra mile. I'll use all the typical methods of phone calls, e-mails, letters, and events at school. But I would make home visits. I've seen the impact of going to the residence of a parent or guardian who tried to make every excuse in the world. Going there gets results. It also shows them that they might as well return your phone call because eventually you'll be at their home, so they can make it simple, or they can wait for the guaranteed knock on their door.

Claire: We always tell ourselves to find the best way to teach the students we have in class this year. I think we have to find the best way to communicate with the parents and guardians each year. And it usually takes more than one method. Electronic methods like e-mail can work, but social networking may also be useful. Old-fashioned letters in the mail may reach some people. Phone calls will get through to some people. Knowing which parent or guardian is most involved in the child's education can be useful. The student's records from elementary school might have a note about the best way to reach the family.

I always try to find out what parents or guardians can do for my classes. One parent works for a chain of restaurants. She could get me coupons for free meals, and I used those as rewards for great work students did. Find out what each parent can do, and put that to use. For the parent or guardian who never replies or who gets belligerent, involve the school administrators or a school counselor. Teachers can deal with most parents, but a few parents have to be dealt with in ways that only a school official can.

I do think that good news is very powerful. Parents and guardians assume that a call or an e-mail will always be about a problem. Tell them the good news, and then if there is a problem later, you already have good rapport and a trust level established.

Reader:

The interview process can include several steps from the application to multiple interviews to a writing task. These are times when a teacher candidate could be asked to prepare and present a lesson. The interview itself could be much longer than the six questions included above, so be fully prepared for the process of interviewing at each school and in each school district you contact.

What did you learn about Nathan, Phillip, and Claire? If one of those three candidates were to be selected for the sixth-grade math position, who should that be and why?

If you were the fourth candidate being interviewed for the position, why should you be selected instead of Nathan, Phillip, or Claire? What have you achieved, what talents do you bring, and how can you persuasively communicate that so the decision is made to select you?

As you read through the interview questions, the answers given by the three candidates, and your answer, was there absolute certainty that you should be a teacher? Was there something less than absolute certainty?

If you choose teaching with total conviction and if teaching reciprocally chooses you with total certainty, the match can be wonderfully symbiotic. If there are doubts, if it is just a job to fall back on, if you were chosen for a job because there were no other applicants or because you could not find anything else, beware of the extra difficulties that factors such as those will bring to a type of work that is challenging even when the match is for all of the right reasons.

"It's my dream to be a teacher. I've always wanted to be a teacher. Working with students looks so interesting to me. I think it will be fun. I know it is a lot of work, but that's true with any real job."

Many teachers prepare for their career, enter their career, and continue throughout their entire teaching career with the dream to make a difference for good in the lives of students. For many of these people, the difficulties, challenges, heartbreaks, frustrations, disappointments, unfair decisions, and other realities of teaching never dominate. The devotion that began the dream and for which the dream inspires and renews is sufficient to withstand the difficulties.

Some other teachers approach teaching with less of the dream and with other motives, some honorable and others dishonorable. The difficulties of the job may just be seen as typical of any job, may be complained about, or may come as no surprise.

Within education is the dream that all students will have outstanding academic achievement. This profession reveres that dream, calling, and purpose. This profession has many people who are deeply dedicated to fulfilling that dream.

Within education are realities that can exhaust, frustrate, disappoint, challenge, and perplex the energy, confidence, and outlook of anyone on a given day. Holding onto the dream can be difficult on the school day or during the school year when everything seems to go wrong no matter what effort you make.

The dream must be nurtured, sustained, and pursued. The reality must be understood, confronted, and mastered. The dream of teaching and the reality of teaching encounter each other in every classroom every day. Of all the variables educators can control, which impact the outcome of dream versus reality, the most significant factor is the teacher. With that in mind, please write profile 7.

PROFILE 7: SHOULD THE READER BE A TEACHER?

Based on what you know about the dream of teaching, the reality of teaching, and yourself, should you be a teacher?

Please think deeply and at length. Then write your profile, and see what the answer is and why that is the answer to the essential question: should I be a teacher?

Chapter Eight

What If?

I always thought I would be a good teacher. I did volunteer work with children when I was in high school. I was a mentor at a middle school during my junior and senior years of college. I did earn my teaching certification by the time I graduated from college, but, I mean, other things came up. I had a great part-time job during college at a car dealership. I knew a lot about computers, so even though it was not my official job, I helped everyone there with computers. They made me a great job offer, more than teaching would have paid. So I took the offer to see what would happen. The owner bought two more dealerships and put me in charge of technology for his entire company. The work is interesting, and the money is great. I can't take a 60 percent pay cut to go be a beginning teacher. Sometimes I wonder what it would have been like to teach, but I doubt I'll ever know. It just didn't work out for me to be a teacher.

My dream was to play professional football. I started playing football when I was five years old. My high school football team was the state runner-up twice during the years I played. I played for two years in college, but some serious injuries meant no more football. If I could not play football, I could coach, so I decided to become a teacher and that way I could coach. What would have happened without those injuries? Well, I did become a teacher and a coach. What amazed me was how similar teaching and coaching were. I actually like teaching as much as coaching, and I think my students learn a lot. So, those college injuries don't bother me much; actually, they don't bother me at all physically. I wonder what if I had been healthy. Would I have played professional football or not? Then I realize that I really like what I do now, so I guess that things just work out the way they are supposed to.

What if I quit after this year? I've taught for six years. I could keep teaching and retire in twenty-four more years. I'd be fifty-three years old then. I could do some other work then, but at age fifty-three, there would not be much opportunity to advance in a career. If I start another job now, when I'm twenty-nine years old, I could spend decades in the next career and really get somewhere. I've taught high school chemistry for six years. One student whom I taught six years ago liked our class so much that in college she majored in physics and minored in chemistry so she could teach both of those subjects. She teaches now at another high school nearby. So I've taught about nine hundred students. I've contributed to our society. What if I keep doing this? I'll teach 3,600 more students in the rest of my teaching years. What if I go do something else, like research for a consumer products company? I have my master's degree in chemistry. I even had an article published about a project my students did on the chemistry of fast food menu items. If I'm going to change jobs, I need to do it now.

What if Mr. James had never been a teacher? What if Mr. James had never been my teacher? Mr. James realized I had writing talent. I never cared for all of the grammar and spelling practice we had to do, but Mr. James knew how to make that interesting. He also realized I had a creative writing style that did not fit in exactly with the common approach to eighth-grade language arts assignments, but Mr. James was flexible so I could write with my style and still show him that I understood everything about grammar and spelling. I won writing awards in high school. I earned several scholarships for writing, and that meant college was almost paid for with the writing scholarships and my straight A high school grades. Thanks to Mr. James, I got serious about school. After college, I earned a master's degree, and now I teach high school English classes. I will start a doctoral program soon and work toward my doctorate while I keep teaching. Someday, I'll teach in college, showing future teachers how to teach. It's all because of Mr. James. I often wonder what I would have been without Mr. James. I would have been fine, but I think I would have known that something was missing.

What if I get through this period by teaching my students the way I wish all of my teachers had taught me? What if I get through all of this disappointment and discouragement by remembering that this is the only chance these students will get to experience third grade. I'm their teacher, and they deserve my best effort. But I'm so frustrated. I was promised two years ago that I would teach third grade just one more year and then I could return to fifth grade, which is my strong preference. Now it looks like I won't see fifth grade for another year, and who knows what reasons I'll hear then for why I have to teach third grade again. Am I asking too much? I know the principal can assign any teacher to any position in the school we are certified for, but, well, what good will it do to keep complaining? Maybe I have to complain. Maybe that's how other people got the grade level they requested. What if I complain until they give in? What if they don't give in? What if they had kept their promise to me?

What if I could afford to change jobs? I'm kidding myself. I've been a teacher for twenty-three years. I can retire after seven more years. I hate to start a seven-year countdown. I can't afford to leave teaching for seven years because of the retirement requirements. I can't leave now because my family needs this steady income and the health insurance I get with this job. What if I moved into school administration? Principals work all year, so that means they make more money. What if I apply for school administrations jobs and I am not selected? When I was in college and decided to become a teacher, I never thought about all of this career stuff or money stuff. It just all seemed like it would work out. What if I had been advised to think through all of the possible ups and downs during a thirty-year teaching career? That's easy to answer. If I had planned all of this when I started teaching, I might not have to figure it out now.

What if every class I teach could be like that one U.S. history class a few years ago? Or like that citizenship class last year? Those were the best classes I ever taught. Is there some way I can get every class to work that hard, pay attention that closely, care so much about learning, behave so well, and completely commit themselves to everything I told them to do? What can I do to make that happen? What if I can make that happen for all of my classes every year? Wow, if I could do that, it would be a dream come true.

What if the people who do not know how to teach and who could never survive in a classroom would quit telling me what to do? If the administrators send us one more e-mail about some form to fill out, some online training we have to complete in a week, or some meeting we have to attend after school today, I'll wonder if my job is to teach or to jump through hoops for the education officials and politicians. What if I could just be left alone in my classroom, without interruptions or e-mail edicts, to really teach my students? That was my original plan, but the reality of teaching is that I have to fight the system so my time with students is not lost to unnecessary stuff.

There are many "what if?" thoughts and questions regarding the experience of a career in teaching or regarding the teaching career that might have been. To analyze and personalize the what-if thoughts and questions further, see which of the following three perspectives about the start of a new school year is closest to how you will think or do think as a new school year's opening day gets very close.

FIRST DAY OF SCHOOL: PERSPECTIVE 1

Next Monday, I get to be a teacher. Next Monday, I get to learn the names of my students, or at least start that process, which sometimes takes a few days.

Next Monday, I get to welcome the students into my classroom and begin the process of making it our classroom.

Next Monday, I get to be a teacher. Oh, I'm always a teacher. At least, if you ask me what work I do, I'll always say, "I'm a teacher," whether I'm asked in October, February, or July.

Next Monday, I get to do the work of a teacher for the first time in over two months. I have enjoyed the summer, but the big part of me that is a teacher was underactive during June and July. I really like the part of me that comes through when I get to teach. Next Monday, the teacher part of me will come fully alive and will stay that way for the entire school year. I have to be with the students for the teacher in me to go from potential to reality.

I get to do the work I always dreamed of doing. Teaching was the answer I always gave as a child when people asked me what I wanted to be when I grew up. I gave the same answer in college when the professor who was advising me asked about my career plan. I told her it was my dream to work with students on their reading skills, thinking skills, writing skills, and everything else that goes with studying English.

Next Monday, I get to be a teacher. This is my third year of teaching. How clearly I remember two years ago. I was hired in early July after I graduated from college in May. I had four interviews in June, and then I heard from two schools—one in my hometown and one in a nearby school district—that I was chosen for a teaching job. I selected the job in the community where I had gone to elementary school through high school. What a thrill to teach in my hometown.

As the first day of my first year of teaching approached, I was so excited, eager, nervous, and impatient. Finally, the first day of school arrived, and I got to be a teacher, sort of. There were forms to fill out and other paperwork that each student had to do. There was not much work done on English until all of the paperwork was finished by each class of students. Finally, we did some reading and we had some discussion. We had some students pay no attention and some pay total attention in my classes. I paid total attention to my students.

I wondered if the students were as excited about getting to be students as I was about getting to be their teacher.

I don't wonder about that now. I realize that I chose to become a teacher. The students are at school because their age and a state law require that. Some students love school, some tolerate school, and some hate school. I get to be the teacher of all of those students. My dream is to inspire all of the students to love learning. The reality is that I was better at that in my second year of teaching than in my first year of teaching. I know that trend will continue this year with more of my students loving to learn than ever before.

Next Monday, I get to be a teacher. I also get to be a teacher next Tuesday and for 178 more teaching days in this school after we complete the first and second days.

Is there ever a day when my attitude declines and I do not think of this as work I get to do but as employment that I have to endure and try to survive? There are difficult days but never so bad that my dream is destroyed.

I get to teach Tasha and Shawn today. I get to teach Martha and Matthew today. I get to learn with my students and from my students. I get to cause learning to happen in the minds of my students.

Getting to teach is, for me, a big part of getting to be who I am and is, for me, a big part of getting to contribute to life itself what I am most qualified to offer.

Next Monday, I get to teach. Until then, I am not fully me. I have a great life, a wonderful family, and dear friends. I'm involved in volunteer work. I have hobbies. I am a well-rounded person. When I get to teach, I'm a better person than when I don't get to teach.

It's not just my job. It's not just what I do to earn a salary. It's not something I thought would be easy. It's not my second or third choice. I very intentionally decided to teach. Teaching also, very intentionally, decided to welcome me.

What if I did not get to teach next Monday, next Tuesday, or ever? Well, I would survive, but because I do get to teach next Monday, I get to live my dream. Will it be difficult? Often. Will it be rewarding? More often. Will it matter? Always. That is another reason I can't wait until next Monday when I get to be a teacher.

FIRST DAY OF SCHOOL: PERSPECTIVE 2

Next Monday, I have to teach. The students return then, so I have to be there and I have to teach. We'll have a lot of typical first-day stuff to do and that will take much of the time in each class. So, there is not much teaching time on Monday. That's fine with me.

This will be my tenth year of teaching. I've been at this middle school for five years. I taught elementary school for five years, but then our district had some population changes and the middle school enrollments went up, so I was moved to middle school.

My first year of middle school, I had to teach eighth-grade science. I prefer to teach sixth graders. I prefer to teach math. Somebody had to teach eighth-grade science. My certification says I am allowed to teach eighth-grade science. I guess there was a shortage, so I had to teach eighth-grade science.

I've asked for sixth-grade math every year, but every year the principal tells me that nobody else is certified at our school to teach eighth-grade science except the people who already teach eighth- or seventh-grade science. The current math teachers have been here longer than I have, and this school seems to make decisions based on seniority. Well, basing that on seniority supports the decisions the administrators wanted to make anyway, and they needed what appeared to be an objective basis like seniority. How will I ever have seniority here?

So, for yet another year, I have to teach eighth-grade science. What's worse than that is having to teach at all. The nine years of my teaching career have not been what I expected. I hear so many excuses being made for students who refuse to work. I hear so many excuses for why the science lab cannot have new equipment and new materials. I hear so many excuses for why some new procedure for taking attendance has to be used one year, only to be replaced the next year and again the next year. So much time gets wasted on dumb stuff like that.

I have to teach this year because my family needs my income and the health care benefits that come with this job. I have to teach this year because other jobs are tough to find. I have to teach this year because what else am I going to start doing this many years into my career?

I have to teach this year and for twenty years after that. When I started teaching, things were better. I liked elementary school more than I like middle school because I got to teach fifth-grade math, which is not too far from what I want to teach now. Then the system began to just put charts and statistics together and just moved us around like boxes in a warehouse. Nobody thought of the teachers getting moved as people. It was clear: accept your new job location or consider your options. What options? I had to teach then, and I have to teach now.

I don't think my request is unreasonable. Let me teach sixth-grade math. I'm a better math teacher than I am a science teacher. I would be better with sixth graders than I am with eighth graders. Why can't this system treat me as well as I am expected to treat my students?

I have to teach next Monday. I don't have a choice. It was not supposed to be like this. It was not like this when I began teaching. Can it ever be that way again when I was excited and inspired? It bothers me that the decisions imposed on me have destroyed my excitement about teaching. The people who made those decisions have difficult jobs, but the way they are doing their job makes my job much more difficult than it has to be for me or for the students.

What if I somehow get excited about eighth-grade science? You tell me how to do that, and I'll give it a try. I don't like walking in the school each day with resentment, frustration, and disappointment. I was not always like that. I'd rather not be that way, but when what you are told to do is the opposite of what you are best at, you either quit or you find a way to do the job well enough to stay employed and to, you hope, give something useful to your students.

It's strange. I really wanted to be a teacher ten years ago. I wish I could really want to be a teacher again. This system has turned me from a teacher who wants to into a teacher who has to. There's got to be a better way.

FIRST DAY OF SCHOOL: PERSPECTIVE 3

I was asked to make a short speech to the rest of the faculty at the Friday morning meeting of our school's teachers, staff members, and school administrators before we finish preparations for the first day of school when students return on Monday.

I almost said no to the request, but who else would do it? I guess I'd rather hear myself talking on Friday at our meeting than have to listen while someone else does the talking. Here's what I said:

Which category are you in? Are you in the group that prefers today to Monday when classes begin for this year? Do you like the opportunities today to ask colleagues about their summer activities; to create the classroom design you want with new posters and a new arrangement of desks; to complete some required paperwork or computer work; to get ahead in making copies of handouts or tests; to update records and accounting information; to send e-mails; to check out videos from the library for use during the first week of school; to update your emergency substitute teachers plans for an unexpected absence; to talk to a school counselor or principal about some concerns of yours with the teaching schedule you have, in general, to get everything organized; and to visit with adults at school?

Or are you in the group that, something like children waiting for Christmas morning, prefers for all of this preliminary preparation to end so the work with students can began? You are eager to open the presents that each student's ideas, mind, personality, hopes, ambitions, problems, and possibilities offer you. Enough of these stacks of materials to go through for the data collection, book rental fees, and assignment of lockers; your real work cannot begin until the students are here. The best part of working at school for you can happen only when you are face to face with students.

It is possible there is a third group that accepts that today has its tasks that must be done, the first day of school will have its tasks that must be done, and every day throughout the school year will have its fill of tasks to complete. Each day is functional. No day is different from any other. There will be problems daily. Some students will learn daily, and some will not. Some decisions by administrators will help you do your job, and others will not. Very little can be done about a lot of this. So the best approach is to do very little beyond the required daily duties, tasks, and obligations.

Do you look at the first day of school as Happy New Year, as summer was too short, or as just another day?

How are students looking at the first day of school? Most students really like summer vacation, but by now, they have done just about everything that could fit into a summer, and they are ready to come here and see their friends. Watch the students on Monday morning as many of them eagerly visit with each other. Will they be just as eager to learn in our classrooms as they were minutes earlier to learn about what their friends have been doing recently? That is up to us.

Our students will be as excited to be in our classrooms as they realize we are excited to have them in our classrooms. Will the words we speak to students and the interaction we have with students on the first day of school convince them it deeply matters to us that we get to be their teacher? Will our words and our interaction convince them we would rather be somewhere else? Will our words and our interactions convince them they are one more generic group that will be given the same generic set of papers and lessons we always use every generic year of teaching?

Whether it is your first year of teaching, your last year of teaching, or a year between those start and stop points, this is the first and only year that your students will experience this grade level in school and these classes in school. We owe the students the best possible new school year.

Think, please, of the best teacher you ever had. Get a clear mental picture of that teacher. The memory may take you to elementary school, to middle school, to high school, to college, to Sunday school, to a camp, or to a mentor of yours. Now identify what that greatest teacher did to so significantly impact you in such good ways that you have vivid, treasured memories now of that dear, important person who touched your life.

Think specifically. Think how she cared for you. Think that she was in her classroom early each day and gave you the extra time and instruction you needed. Yes, she cared, but think of the actions she took to implement caring.

The truth is we know what great teachers have done through the ages. Those actions still work now. On Monday and every day, we can be the greatest teacher our students ever have.

Yes, our work becomes more demanding every year. Yes, the education bureaucracy sends us more paperwork and other stuff that does little or no good for what matters most. Yes, society expects schools to solve every problem impacting children and teenagers. That is reality. We cannot change that reality, but we can keep it from changing us.

Our greatest teachers did not let the education bureaucracy or the point-less meetings they had to attend or the disappointing decisions made by school officials keep them from being great teachers who made sure we learned.

Our greatest teachers held onto the dream that they could touch lives of students. Our greatest teachers mastered the realities of their work so they could experience with their students the dream of genuinely teaching. Our greatest teachers were a brilliant, dynamic, sensible mixture of 51 percent dream and 49 percent reality. Both parts were necessary, but the dream part had to be larger. The reality was the foundation to build on. The dream was the purpose, the reason, the goal, and the steps taken each day to cause learning, to touch lives, and to make a difference.

All of us are employed for this school year. We will get paid twice each month. School begins on Monday for everyone. Or does it? Will the work, interaction, and activities in our classrooms on Monday be as good as or better than what our greatest teachers provided for us when we were students? I encourage you to use that standard. Teach your students as well or better than your best teacher taught you. The results are magnificent for students and for teachers. Why settle for anything less than that?

What if every classroom in this school has the attitude, atmosphere, dream, and reality that what happens here every day will be as good as or better than what happened in the classroom of our greatest teacher? That dream can be our school's reality. That dream can be your classroom's reality. That dream can be your student's reality. That dream can be your reality. School starts Monday. Happy New Year.

What if the new school year is anything but happy? What if there are more problems confronting each teacher than one person can solve? What if the students do not obey rules, follow instructions, and do the work?

What if the school's air conditioning breaks on August days when the temperature is ninety-five degrees outside and seems to feel like that inside? What if the school enrollment is up unexpectedly, and class sizes average thirty-three students per class in classrooms designed for twenty-seven students per class?

What if many decisions at school are based on seniority, and as a new teacher you end up with everything that no other teacher asked for? You have the classes no one else would teach. You have the before-school and after-school duties no one else would do. You have to float from classroom to classroom. What if the seniority reality is that it will take many years before any of this changes?

What if the principal of the school makes decisions that you oppose? What if students receive minimal punishment when you write discipline referrals? What if you are told to use more technology in your teaching methods, but the technology equipment and system at school is outdated and often does not work?

What if the budget for textbooks is reduced to zero for two consecutive years? What if teacher salaries are frozen for two consecutive years? What if the teacher retirement system begins to have difficulty with its financial obligations? What if the financial responsibilities you have to your family are more than your teacher income can pay for?

What if the decision-making process at your school and at your school district involves little or no input from teachers? What if politicians continue to pass laws telling teachers to make every student a scholar?

What if some students bring weapons to school? What if some students buy, sell, or use drugs at school? What if the school building has places where students know it is easy to hide, misbehave, and never get noticed?

What if you have a class of thirty-three students, many or most of whom have severe allergy conditions, asthma problems, other health issues, learning disabilities, and emotional difficulties, and you are required to accommodate each of these realities, although you are not a nurse, physician, psychologist, or psychiatrist?

What if everything that can go wrong one day actually does go wrong? What if that happens two consecutive days? What if the people whom you ask for help tell you there is not much they can do or tell you their job is even more difficult than your job?

What if the tests you gave in several classes today will take fifteen hours to grade, and the tests in your other classes later this week will take ten hours to grade? What if this is a typical week?

What if the students cheat? What if students use vulgar language in class? What if students skip school? What if students are arrested for shoplifting on Saturday and are in your classroom on Monday?

What if the student who struggled with reading begins making great improvement because you asked a colleague for an idea, you tried the suggestion, and it worked?

What if you receive an e-mail from a former student saying,

> Hi. Remember me from seventh-grade math class about ten years ago? I wanted you to know I'm graduating from college soon, and I'll work for an accounting company starting in June. It was your teaching that got me interested in math. Because of what you did for me, I majored in math and accounting in college, and I have accepted a great job offer. Thank you so much. You are the best teacher I ever had.

What if a student's father who works for a computer company arranges to donate some used laptop computers from a client of his who was replacing their old laptops? What if that parent arranges to donate those computers for your classroom because of the outstanding learning experience his daughter is having in your class?

What if the lesson plans you put extra effort into work better than you expected because the students respond with so much interest and with so many ideas there is not enough time in one day to complete all of these newly emerging thoughts? What if the continuation of this lesson on the next day works even better?

What if you give a musically talented student the opportunity to prepare and perform a song in class? The song is his original creation and is all about the scientific periodic table. What if the song is as academically valid as an essay on or an analysis of the periodic table? What if the unique talents of other students are applied in future assignments?

What if a student nominates you for a teaching award? What if the letter she wrote to nominate you brings tears to your eyes and pure joy to your heart?

What if you decide that, although teaching well is exhausting, you promise yourself to get proper exercise daily, eat nutritious food only, always have a portion of each day set aside as quiet time for you, and read the great book you have promised yourself you will read?

What if you start saying no to optional duties you are asked to accept? The dance will be chaperoned without you, and the sleep you get while the dance goes late into the night will make you more prepared to teach. Do you miss every dance or other activity? No. Do you attend every dance and every other school activity? Double no.

What if the lessons you prepare for your classes go very well today, the computers work, the grades on yesterdays test in one class were their best grades yet, there are few PA interruptions of your classes, and attendance in your classes is better than usual?

What if, at the end of a school year, you know, absolutely know, that you did everything one teacher could do for the students? What if that reality convinces you that enough progress was made in this school year to show that the dream of teaching can come true, in small steps, one student at a time, and one class at a time, despite days, weeks, or months that make the reality seem stronger than the dream? What if this year of teaching has enough times of success that you anticipate the next year of teaching with renewed devotion, commitment, enthusiasm, and new knowledge of what works?

What if the dream of teaching shapes the reality of teaching? What if the reality of teaching is mastered so the dream of teaching can endure, prevail, and, with increasing frequency, thrive?

Teaching is demanding and fascinating, teaching is exhausting and inspiring, teaching is frustrating and encouraging, and teaching is heartbreaking and life changing. Teaching is a combination of dream and reality.

It would be sad to live a life of wondering, "What if I had been a teacher? I think I would have been really good at that. It just never worked out."

It would be sad to live a life of wondering, "What if I had not been a teacher? I had that other job offer and that company has grown. People there are making so much money. I can't quit teaching now, but I wonder what might have been."

Because teaching is a combination of dream and reality, the decision to become a teacher applies heart and soul to the dream of teaching, while applying mind and body to the reality of teaching.

Your heart may shout, "I just love children." Your mind may shout back, "Yeah, you love the children you babysit for. That's different from being in a school, being in a classroom, and being with thirty children who are your students, not the children you take to movies or the playground when you babysit."

Once a person becomes a teacher, the decision to continue throughout a career as a teacher is a combination of the original reasons that led you to teach and new reasons—marriage, children, income, other opportunities, or no other opportunities.

The dream of teaching and the reality of teaching exist now and will exist forever. Whether you enter that dream and reality and whether you stay for one year, ten years, or a career in that dream and reality will be a deeply personal decision. Among the factors to consider in making those decisions is "What if."

Epilogue

"Deborah, it's great to see you. How is everything?"

"Good, everything is good. Work is so hard, but, you know, I like it a lot. I mean, the pay is good, and the people I work with are great. So, Jessica, How about you?"

"I'm teaching ninth- and tenth-grade English at Lincoln High School in my hometown. It's where I went to high school, so I knew some of the people there. What about you and Thomas? You know, you were so serious during our senior year in college. I thought the big news at our first college homecoming would be that Deborah and Thomas are engaged. So, tell me."

"Jessica, we got engaged in June, but we are more than engaged. We're getting married the Saturday after Thanksgiving. I'm so excited. The invitations go out next week. It's all by e-mail and Internet, so you'll get your e-invitation. Please, please come to our wedding; you have to be there."

"Deborah, I would not miss your wedding for anything. I know I'll have a lot of schoolwork to do over Thanksgiving, but I'll be at your wedding. That is so exciting."

"Yeah, there's Thomas. He went to talk to some of our old professors. Thomas is teaching middle school math. I thought about teaching, but, you know, my family has the business that my father wants me to run. The people there are great, and the business has been a success forever. Daddy wants to retire soon, so in a few years I might run the place."

"Hello, Jessica. Good to see you. Deborah told you, right? We're getting married. It's going to be perfect. Be sure to come."

"I'll be there, Thomas. I'll take a break from grading papers and planning lessons so I can be at the wedding event of the year. So, how is teaching going for you, Thomas? Do you like it?"

Deborah walked away for a few minutes to talk with other members of her very recently graduating class from college. Last May was college graduation. Five months later was their first college homecoming. Much had happened in that short time. Jessica added to her question before Thomas could respond.

"Teaching high school is so much harder than I thought it would be. I mean, you never get caught up: papers to grade, discipline referrals, meetings, and computer stuff. I thought we worked hard in college, Thomas, but this is twice as much."

Thomas knew the feeling. "Yeah, middle school is the same. I work hard, but it's never enough. The experienced teachers give me some ideas when I ask. I pretty much just try to keep up. I sponsor the chess club and I help coach the volleyball team, plus Deborah and I have all the wedding plans."

Jessica asked Thomas the question she sometimes asked herself. "Are you glad you decided to teach?"

Thomas was honest. "Most of the time. Not always. I wonder if I can make enough money so, when Deborah and I have children, we'll be able to afford everything. She's working for her father and she can keep doing that, but when we have children, she wants to stay at home with them. So, I don't know. I like the students and most parts of the job, but I don't know if I can do this forever. I'll just take it one year at a time. How about you, Jessica?"

Jessica was also honest but somewhat more hopeful. "I'm glad to be a teacher most of the time, also. I mean, my students do pretty good work. I think they will eventually do even better work. I'm learning so much about what to do and what not to do. The English classes I took in college help a lot. The education classes, you know, I never use that stuff. It was interesting, but it's not practical. When thirty tenth graders need to write better paragraphs, the books we read about theories of learning are not much help. But I like being a teacher. It's the job I always had in mind. It's what my college education was all about. I spend about sixty or sixty-five hours each week on school, so teaching is a big part of who I am. I sure don't spend sixty or sixty-five other hours each week on anything else, sleep included."

"Well, Jessica, hang in there. It's hard work, but we can figure it out. I'm going to talk with some of our professors with Deborah. Great to see you, Jessica."

"Great to see you, Thomas. Congratulations on the engagement and the wedding. I'll see the happy couple at your wedding next month."

"Deborah, it's great to see you. How have you been? I think the last time we saw you was the fifth reunion. Now it's the twentieth. Can you believe it has been twenty years since we graduated from college? Tell me all about you. Thomas, come join us."

Thomas was glad to join his wife of almost twenty years and their good friend from college, Jessica.

"Well, I'm doing fine. I'm in my twentieth year of teaching high school English. I started with ninth and tenth graders. Then about ten years ago I moved to eleventh and twelfth graders. I also teach some dual-credit classes the high school seniors take for both high school and college credit. And I finally finished my doctorate. The classes went fast. I finished them in less than three years, but the dissertation took three more years and really was a slow process. Teaching full time and working on the doctorate filled every minute of the day, but it's been worth it."

"Dr. Jessica, that's fantastic. You really do take this teaching stuff seriously!" Thomas said enthusiastically.

"I do. With twenty years invested in education, I can see myself doing this for twenty more years. Why stop? The students are doing great work, and each year brings some new challenge or new adventure. Now tell me about both of you."

Deborah began, "We have three children, two daughters aged eighteen and sixteen. Our son is fourteen. They love school. You would be impressed with their grades. I work part time at the family business my father started years ago. And Thomas works there full time." Jessica had not known that Thomas was no longer a teacher.

Thomas explained, "I stayed in teaching for six years. I liked it and was good at it, but with two children then and a third child on the way, finances were getting stretched. Deborah and I had promised each other that she would be a stay-at-home mother. We did everything we could, but the teacher pay was about half of what I could make managing the business, so we made that change. With the oldest child going to college next year, it's a good thing we started saving seriously for college fourteen years ago when I changed jobs. How about you, Jessica? What kept you in teaching all these years? And the doctorate on top of that. What's the secret of your staying power?"

Jessica knew the answer but so did many other teachers. The answer is not a secret, but it is understood better by some people than by others.

Jessica explained, "You probably learn something new about your children every day. Being mother and father to your children is a big part of who you are as a couple and as individuals. You probably see something new in your business every day. Managing that company has challenges and opportunities, but you go back each day ready to succeed."

"For me, no two years of teaching have been alike. I learn something new, hear something new, or see something new, if I am paying attention properly, every day. I have not done the same job each year for twenty identical years. I've been a teacher for twenty very different years with different students each year. Not just different groups of students each year but different personalities, interests, strengths, weaknesses, problems, skills, and ambitions. So, being a teacher continues to fascinate me."

Deborah wondered, "Sometimes I'm exhausted taking care of our three teenagers. You teach big groups of teenagers all the time. It must exhaust you. What keeps you going?"

Jessica smiled and said, "The same work that exhausts me also inspires me. Taking care of your children does exhaust you, but you don't define parenthood by the occasional fatigue. You define parenthood by the wonder of it all, the joys, the achievements, and the working together to solve problems and make good things happen. Sure, teaching exhausts me, but I do not define my job by how tired it makes me. I define teaching by how eagerly I accept the challenges and by how well I get the desired results. Teaching is so much more than a job to me. Teaching is a big part of who I am."

Thomas had noticed something as Jessica talked. "Did you marry a teacher?"

Everyone smiled. Jessica answered, "Of course. We met when we were working on our doctorates. Paul is somewhere around here. I think he saw a professor he knows from some organization they both belong to. He'll be back in a minute, and I'll introduce you. It is so good to see both of you again. Let's not wait five, ten, or more years until our next conversation."

Whenever that next conversation does happen, it will include some updates about the three children in Deborah and Thomas's family. The conversation will include an update on Thomas's business. The conversation will include a lot of comments from Jessica about her recent experiences as a teacher.

Most of Jessica's stories about teaching will be favorable, positive, and encouraging because her dream of teaching continues to come true, mostly true, year after year. Some of Jessica's stories about teaching will include the challenges, problems, and difficulties of teaching because such realities continue to confront teachers, year after year.

Jessica's dream of teaching does not ignore, overlook, blame, or sugarcoat the reality of teaching. Jessica's dream of teaching sufficiently energizes, inspires, informs, and guides her so she can master the realities.

Among the reasons that Jessica became a teacher, has been a teacher for twenty years, and will continue to teach for many years is that teaching is not merely Jessica's job. Teaching is a big part of who Jessica always intended to be, of who Jessica is, and of who Jessica will continue to be. She would have it no other way. Life would have it no other way. Teaching is Jessica's dream, and teaching is Jessica's reality.

About the Author

Keen J. Babbage has twenty-six years of experience as a teacher and administrator in middle school, high school, college, and graduate school. He is the author of *911: The School Administrator's Guide to Crisis Management* (1996), *Meetings for School-Based Decision Making* (1997), *High-Impact Teaching: Overcoming Student Apathy* (1998), *Extreme Teaching* (2002), *Extreme Learning* (2004), *Extreme Students* (2005), *Results-Driven Teaching: Teach So Well That Every Student Learns* (2006), *Extreme Economics* (2007, 2009), *What Only Teachers Know about Education* (2008), *Extreme Writing* (2010), and *The Extreme Principle* (2010).

Breinigsville, PA USA
01 April 2011
258988BV00002B/3/P